# Veil of Miracles

## CHIARA'S JOURNEY

Helen Barr

First published 2018

Text copyright © Helen Barr 2018
The moral right of the author has been asserted

Mary MacKillop photos used with permission of the Trustees of the Sisters of St Joseph and must not be reproduced without permission.

Cover design by Helen Barr, artwork created by Sonya Murphy
Internal design and typesetting by Sonya Murphy, Adala Publishing

All rights reserved. Without limiting the rights under copyright reserved above, no part of this publication may be reproduced, stored in or introduced into a retrieval system, or transmitted, in any form or by any means (electronic, mechanical, photocopying, recording or otherwise) without the prior written permission of Helen Barr, the copyright owner of this book.

ISBN 978-0-646-99416-1
ISBN 978-0-646-99433-8

To order additional copies of this book, email arkerup@bigpond.com or order through the facebook site www.facebook.com/Veil-of-miracles

*Dedicated to*

Mr Ahmad Hanieh (Deceased)

Dr Rasiah Vigneswaran (Deceased)

Dr John O'Loughlin

Dr Nik Vrodos

and their families

# *Contents*

Acknowledgements .................................................................. ix
Introduction ........................................................................... 1
Part One
    Where to begin .................................................................. 5
    Enter the salesman ........................................................... 10
    The pregnancy ................................................................. 12
    Royal Adelaide Hospital .................................................. 18
    An abominable act ........................................................... 21
    Queen Victoria Hospital Adelaide ................................... 24
    The whisper ..................................................................... 30
    The birth .......................................................................... 33
    Neo-Natal Intensive Care Unit ........................................ 37
    Only a miracle can save her ............................................. 45
    Chiara's rainbow .............................................................. 49
    First cuddle ...................................................................... 52
    Neurosurgery trauma begins ........................................... 57
    All babies are tiny ............................................................ 63
    Two hospitals unite ......................................................... 66
    Home at last ..................................................................... 77

## Part Two

| | |
|---|---|
| A mother's intuition | 83 |
| Expect the unexpected | 85 |
| A father's denial | 92 |
| Intermittent shunt blockages | 95 |
| One step forward two steps back | 105 |
| Special kisses | 109 |
| Complications continue | 113 |
| My consolation | 122 |
| Free wheel…ing | 124 |
| Jason | 127 |
| The nightmare continues | 130 |
| Chiara starts school | 140 |
| One shunt or two | 143 |
| A special Christmas service | 148 |
| Wishes come true | 151 |
| History repeats itself | 164 |

## Part Three

| | |
|---|---|
| Mary MacKillop | 173 |
| The beatification | 178 |
| The flower girl | 187 |
| Penola | 190 |
| Visions continue | 196 |
| From celebrations to commiserations | 198 |
| Mary MacKillop's second miracle | 203 |
| The Novena | 205 |
| Our world explodes | 209 |

| | |
|---|---|
| Changing doctors and direction | 213 |
| Flinders Medical Centre Adelaide | 216 |
| Life goes on | 223 |
| Uncanny coincidences | 226 |
| Sudden accidents change lives | 230 |
| Intuition ignored | 232 |
| Planning a future | 238 |
| Fighting for improvements | 241 |
| Euthanasia | 246 |
| Epilogue: An extraordinary journey | 248 |
| Thank you | 253 |
| Glossary | 258 |

# *Acknowledgements*

Danielle my precious unique daughter and adored sister of Chiara. Thank you for your extraordinary patience, understanding and encouragement. The remarkable confidence you have shown in your sister has been an inspiration to us all. I am exceedingly proud of you and thank you for my cherished, precious grandchildren, Braeden, Tayah, Jai and Ashton. I love you all more than life itself.

Laurel and Allan, my treasured parents, I could not have coped without your unconditional love and support throughout my life. You were always there for me and because of you, together we raised two perfect children who will forever adore and cherish you both.

My siblings Teresa, Greg, Trevor and your families, along with aunts, uncles and cousins, I extend my eternal gratitude to you all for all your love and support throughout the years.

My team of supportive and loving long time friends, you all know who you are, my heartfelt and loving thanks to each and every one of you.

Phyllis Marjorie Shergis (deceased) a former employer and treasured friend. As your personal assistant in 1972 you taught me, as a seventeen-year-old that regardless of what happens in life, *'it could be worse.'* Those four words had an enormous impact, helping me withstand events that have since shaped my life. I have absolutely no doubt, that single most valuable piece of advice given so long ago, has at times been the ultimate saviour of my sanity.

Bob Whitington (deceased). We came to you as strangers yet you took the time to care. You read my original manuscript long before much had even happened and declared, 'This story must be told.' Thank you for giving me the encouragement I needed to continue writing.

Robert Thomas you entered my life when I first began this book and seeing me struggling with a typewriter arrived on my doorstep with a Laptop, and provided lessons on how to use it. I shall be forever grateful for the friendship you offered and exceptional patience. Without you this book may never have come to fruition, and I would probably still be computer illiterate.

Steve as you gently eased away the heartache and wiped away the tears you restored my faith, my confidence, my self-esteem. You taught me to laugh again, to feel again, to trust again; to love again while bringing peace, happiness, and fulfilment into my life.

Thank you for wanting us, thank you for needing us.

Mary MacKillop thank you for infiltrating our lives<br>
restoring my faith, ensuring<br>
I and many others now<br>
Believe in Miracles

# *Introduction*

When asked to write a book recounting my tiny premature daughter's struggle throughout her first four years I didn't realise we had already embarked on an extraordinary, and at times, paranormal journey that would have this book continually writing itself as we lived through her struggle.

At twenty-eight week's gestation in a haze of desperation and despair we entered a world I had no knowledge of. Determined to survive, Chiara's life immediately became a cruel second-by-second existence. Within her first twenty-four hours she battled septicaemia (blood poisoning) severe lung disease and a massive brain haemorrhage (bleed) and by the tenth day was suffering hydrocephalus (water on the brain). We left hospital one hundred and one days later with a grim prognosis.

By her fourth year Chiara had fought blood poisoning, lung disease, brain haemorrhage, hydrocephalus, cysts at the base of her brain, meningitis, pseudomonas, pneumonia, surgical decompression of her skull, seizures and third and sixth nerve palsy. A ventricular peritoneal shunt inserted into her brain ten days after her birth, she underwent her 50th neurosurgical shunt revision on her fifteenth birthday.

## Introduction

One week prior to the beatification of Mary MacKillop, Chiara informed me she had a strange dream and I realised something inexplicable had transpired.

I offer our story to the best of my recollection and understanding, written as we have lived it, in anticipation of providing consolation and support to others, while extending eternal gratitude to the brilliant, dedicated medical and nursing teams across many South Australian hospitals, both public and private who treat us with proficiency and compassion.

I write without prejudice, yearning for an improved, re-engineered hospital system that ensures on-going first-rate, quality care and attention whilst providing the best available technology and equipment, with zero tolerance of egotistical staff and has been written the only way I know how, from the heart.

If reliving the sometimes harrowing nightmare to write this book provides hope and inspiration to just one person or leads to change then it has been worth the torment and anguish.

*Helen M Barr*

# PART ONE

# *Where to begin*

'Helen Dr O'Loughlin will see you now.'

'Thank you Sue.' My regular gynaecological check-up due I entered the room with the beautifully polished antique desk. Looking serious at me over the top of his half-moon glasses Dr O'Loughlin stands to greet me. 'Helen it's great to see you you're looking well.'

'Thank you I feel well for a ch...'

'Helen I want to know how you're still sane.'

'Pardon, sane?'

'You breeze in here, and after all you've been through you have a smile on your face. I treat so many incredibly stressed women yet none of them have been through what you have, and you're the one who always walks in smiling. I need to know how you do it and furthermore, I want to see it written in a book so I can refer people to it.' In a state of shock I started to laugh. 'Sane. Me. Am I? Oh you can't be serious. I can't write a book I only ever got C's for essays in school.'

'Helen you must, it would help so many others. Please consider it.'

'But where would I start? Where does Chiara's story begin and how would I finish it? What would I write for a final chapter when I don't even know what's in store?' My smile fading it was soon clear why he wanted Chiara's story told. My instant reaction was one of horror. He was asking me not only to relive a nightmare but to put it all into words. The emotions and memories I had buried for so long began scrambling through my mind.

Gathering my thoughts and hoping my anguish wasn't obvious, I felt bewildered and became distressed at the thought of reliving everything we had been through. Gazing despairingly into his eyes I knew I would oblige but didn't know how, or where, to begin or finish. The fact that for over twenty years Dr O'Loughlin had always been there for me more than justified his request. He for the first time was asking something of me.

Perplexed I blurted out, 'Sane? You want to know how I'm still sane, well if I *am* it's only because I have people like you, Dr Vigneswaran and Mr Hanieh who've had faith in Chiara and me. You have all embraced and supported us, so how could I let any of you down. How could I let my daughters down? Besides, there are many people far worse off, and after all you've done for me I don't have the right to give up. Otherwise, what would it have all been for?'

No-one knew there were times when I was overcome with helplessness and feelings of failure and I contemplated the easy way out. But where would that have left my two precious daughters? I couldn't do it to them. I had to dig deep within my tortured soul, and find the strength to continue. There wasn't any other alternative than to accept what we had been dealt.

As the initial shock of being asked to write a book began to subside, it became obvious Dr O'Loughlin wasn't aware how much Chiara had suffered since I last saw him. I realised he was only referring to her first three months of life. By the time this conversation took place in 1991, she was four years old and had undergone neurosurgery numerous times since birth. None of her doctors dared to chance a prognosis. As I endeavoured to bring him up to date a look of horror enveloped his face as again he repeated, 'Helen this story *must* be written.'

An eerie sense of calm flowed through my veins. From the moment Chiara was born gravely ill I believed her life would have a profound significance. I could never have imagined what was to unfold, or that I would be asked to write a book about the impact her birth had on our lives, in order to help others.

After a great deal of soul-searching to determine how to start this book, I ultimately realised Chiara's story begins with the birth of my first baby, Danielle. In 1973 while working for Shergis Hairdressers in Adelaide as Mrs Shergis' Secretary, I married and at the age of eighteen gave birth to my first child. Enduring morning sickness from the day I conceived until the day my precious daughter was born I was prescribed Debbendox tablets which had been deemed safe to use while pregnant.

It took two tablets in the morning and one at night to control the vomiting. I don't know how I would have managed without them and was surprised a few years later when they were withdrawn from the market, apparently blamed for birth defects. I took three tablets a day for the entire pregnancy so perhaps we were just lucky. Despite the morning sickness and Debbendox, Danielle was born healthy in September 1973, weighing in at seven pounds. She would be referred to throughout her life as Dani.

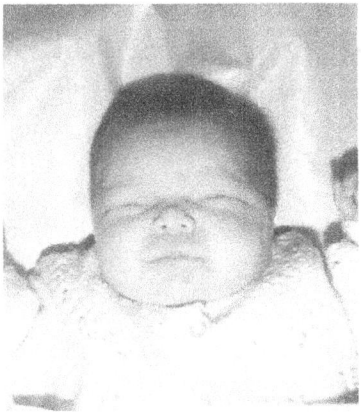

*Danielle One Day Old 1973*

With Dani only six weeks old Mrs Shergis knocked on our door pleading with me to return to work. I picked Dani up out of the bassinette insisting I couldn't leave her, particularly at such a young age. Mrs Shergis smiled, asked for a cuddle, and said she would look after her. I returned to work the following week taking Dani with me.

I didn't realise working for Mrs Shergis would have a massive impact on my life. I'll never forget the day I answered a phone call from a panicked hairdresser whose client's hair had turned orange, and I didn't know how to tell Mrs Shergis.

Expecting her to be upset when I broke the news, instead she handed Dani to me and calmly replied, 'Tell her I'm on my way dear and not to worry, *it could be worse.*' From that day forward those four words continue to resonate throughout the lows of my life, and I often hear myself repeating them to others whenever something goes wrong.

***

Six months later my then husband was transferred to Whyalla, approximately five hours from Adelaide. It left me no choice but to resign from the job I loved, to live in a small caravan with a young baby, isolated approximately 400 kilometres from family and friends. We were assured the contract would only be for six weeks. As the months passed and the heat of summer arrived, without air-conditioning I was constantly wetting towels to keep Dani cool. After the sixth month I had enough and returned home; with her father following shortly after.

***

Over the next twelve months I struggled with excruciating pain and nausea while my marriage was falling apart. Desperately ill I sought help from a local General Practitioner. I saw him numerous times only to have him continually blaming 'the Pill.' He kept prescribing different brands and strengths for me to try.

Unable to tolerate the pain any longer, and my intuition telling me it had nothing to do with 'the Pill,' I insisted on a referral to see my gynaecologist Dr O'Loughlin. It took him barely a few minutes to declare I either had an ovarian cyst or a pregnancy in the tube. 'Dr O'Loughlin if I'm pregnant then I have been for the last twelve months, so it must be a cyst. I feel really ill.'

Agreeing it was more likely a cyst he booked surgery for the following week giving me strict instructions not to hesitate to contact him should the pain worsen. Returning home I was relieved the agony would soon disappear but within days I was violently ill so my husband took me to my parent's house while he went to work.

Two hours later my mother phoned Dr O'Loughlin apologising for interrupting him while he was in an operating theatre. On his advice, and without hesitation, she drove me to the Queen Victoria Hospital where he would be there to meet us. Not surprisingly he discovered a haemorrhaging cyst on my right ovary the size of a grapefruit. He removed the ovary and cyst, marking the beginning of numerous gynaecological operations to span the next twenty years.

By 1975 my tumultuous marriage had ended, the divorce finalised two years later. Alone with an 18-month-old child my world was in turmoil. All I wanted was a healthy happy baby and the marriage I had dreamed of. I learned through experience how to cope, finding the courage and strength to support my daughter alone, with help from my parents and siblings. I faced life as a single parent to the best of my ability. I worked casual and flexible hours, mainly in the field of Market Research, or as a Console Operator or Book-keeper which enabled me to be at home for Dani before and after school.

Over the years I averaged at least one gynaecological operation every twelve months and also developed endometriosis, a disorder causing the lining of the womb to break away attaching itself to internal organs causing a great deal of pain and discomfort.

On diagnosing endometriosis, Dr O'Loughlin expressed cautiously, 'Helen knowing your history I doubt you'll ever be able to conceive again but I can't and won't play God. I'll give you a one per cent chance but it would be a miracle if you ever do have another baby.'

## *Enter the salesman*

In 1985 ten years after my divorce, with Dani at the age of twelve, I hoped to improve and secure our financial future. I didn't know how or what I was going to do but I didn't want to do it solo. After a great deal of consideration I realised the ideal person to involve in a new venture was my ex sister-in-law, and close friend Judy.

Together with her husband Sam we enjoyed our friendship, and saw no reason to end it simply because my marriage to Sam's brother ended in divorce. Judy agreed we could possibly achieve mutual success so with two heads brainstorming it became a process of elimination eventually realising there are two major areas in which to make money; food and children.

We decided to focus on children knowing if we could invent an item children wanted we would have to be on a winner. Finally we hit on it recognising there was a market not catered for, and after many days and long nights we produced a prototype. We then applied for, and received a Government Grant told we were sitting on a gold mine with huge potential. Our product ready to package, we arranged for a sales representative from a local cardboard packaging company to visit us.

Our new business venture launched at an expo in Adelaide coincided with the first Australian Grand Prix. We were on our way to success, and life was looking the most promising it ever had. We designed an all Australian family of dolls which were suitable for children to play with or as Australian souvenirs.

The range included a swagman and Aussie Father Christmas on the back of a kangaroo, through to Australi Anna and Australi Adam dressed in green and gold shirt and overalls, carrying their own passports and also Jill Aroo and Jack Aroo dressed in denim overalls and checked shirts complete with felt hats with corks. Each doll was individually hand-made and we lodged trademarks and registered the business.

Over the course of the following week there were numerous telephone calls from Gary the salesman from the packaging company; always business based yet strangely never important. Frequent appointments followed which soon led to almost daily visits. We were certainly receiving personalised attention but when the packaging was delivered I presumed the telephone calls and visits would cease. His persistence set in motion an ill-fated relationship doomed for disaster.

The visits and telephone calls continued, taking on a more personal line of approach with such endearing well-worn lines as *where have you been all my life* and *I can't live without you.* Then came the part about an unhappy marriage and how it was *me* he wanted to spend the rest of his life with, that his marriage was over and only a matter of time before everything would be finalised.

A year later I thought I had against my better judgement, fallen in love. It was the last thing I wanted after having my share of broken dreams and promises, lies, heartache, and violent relationships so why should I believe him. Why would *he* be any different but conscious I had to trust somebody sometime, I settled into a seemingly happy relationship.

Gary continued declaring his love. We discussed wedding plans and knowing he wanted to be a father, and the fact I may never conceive again was an issue often discussed, with his attitude always adamant, if we are meant to have children we will.

# *The pregnancy*

January 1987 began with an incomprehensible feeling I was pregnant, even though I had long before accepted I would never bear another child, instinctively I *knew* I was pregnant. I made an appointment with our family practitioner, Dr Leaney who saved my life at six weeks of age when my mother took me to him for a second opinion after being told by another doctor that I only had a cold. Dr Leaney soon declared, 'this baby hasn't got any blood' and treated me for anaemia.

Intense emotions engulfing me, I convinced myself he would diagnose a case of wishful thinking and almost cancelled the appointment, before my day of reckoning arrived. Sitting on the edge of the chair impatiently awaiting the analysis of my urine sample, I watched as he held the small disc between his fingers slowly rocking it from side to side. Eyes transfixed on his face I dared not miss the first sign of any result, and after what seemed an eternity, the silence was broken.

A look of astonishment on his face he said softly, 'It seems the result shows positive. Of course you realise these tests aren't always correct, and Helen with your history it's highly unlikely you would be pregnant. I'll send a blood test to the laboratory and you can come back tomorrow for the confirmed results but don't get your hopes up, because it would take a miracle.'

Satisfied the urine test was incorrect I left, scolding myself for wasting Dr Leaney's time. A pregnancy wasn't possible, what was I thinking. I would return tomorrow, if for no other reason than to complete a wasted exercise, conclusively putting any thought of a pregnancy behind me.

Seated in the waiting room the next day, I picked up a magazine. Unable to concentrate on reading, I had an urge to walk out, get in the car and drive home. I couldn't have any more children so what was I doing there?

As I was about to leave I heard, 'Helen come through.' I followed the nursing sister down the corridor to the open doorway. 'Hello Helen, take a seat I'll be with you in a minute, I'll just get your test results.' Dr Leaney seemed to take forever but it was no doubt barely a matter of minutes. He sat down, pulling his chair in close to his desk. Opening the results, he leaned back, took a deep breath and said, 'Helen your test has come back positive!' I will never forget that moment and I'm not sure who was more stunned, him or me. Dr Leaney stared at the test results as we both sat in silence for a moment.

Reaffirming his belief my chances of ever becoming pregnant were next to zero, he admitted he was convinced I would never again conceive. I asked for a referral to return to my gynaecologist Dr O'Loughlin, and in a state of shock left the surgery. The immediate effect impossible to describe, flopping into the car I sat motionless staring into space, trying to comprehend what the news meant to me, Dani, Gary and our families.

After a short while, the elation was overwhelming. I was going to have a baby. Me! It had taken years to accept I would never have another child and I was bursting with emotion as I tried to absorb the most astounding, almost frightening news. Fourteen years had passed since giving birth to Dani and now she would be presented with a brother or sister, who would change our lives forever.

I wondered what she would think and how her friends and their families would react. Little did I realise how much support I would receive from everyone. I thought of Gary; was it *really* what he wanted? When I arrived home he was sitting on the front doorstep waiting for me. I told him he was about to become a father and he appeared euphoric, looking into my eyes, holding my head in his hands, he kept repeating, 'I don't believe it, I'm going to be a dad, I'm going to be a dad!' Reassuring me of his undying love and devotion we settled down to ponder and plan a future together.

Taking my hand he told me emphatically he wanted to be totally free of all 'hassles' with his wife and settle the divorce with the utmost urgency. He told me he would need a couple more months, and there wasn't any need for me to worry. We would marry before the year was out. I had no reason to doubt his word.

Had we been married my parents would have been delighted but already raising one child as a single parent, they didn't want to see me struggling to raise another. Believing I had full comprehension of what lay ahead with our future secure, I decided the time was right to tell Dani. To say she was shocked would be an understatement, and her attitude toward Gary changed. They had developed a friendly rapport but in an instant the alliance that had once existed between them had disintegrated, never to be revived. It broke my heart.

Gary insisted he should be the one to tell my parents and reassure them of his intentions. He promised to look after their daughter and her children forever. With grave reservations, they remained unconvinced. Wanting to trust him, something was tearing at them out of concern for me, Dani, and now unborn grandchild.

A month later, saying he'd almost finished finalising his marital affairs, Gary informed me he would be moving in with us within a fortnight. I was prepared to wait for as long it took, not wanting the problems an unresolved marriage could bring into our new life.

The fortnight came and went with him muttering he needed more time. There had been a hitch with his wife determined to keep the family home, and apparently her parents were helping to buy him out.

Determined not to start again with nothing, *he* wanted to keep the house whatever the cost and would 'work it out.' My head was telling me what my heart didn't want to hear.

\*\*\*

The day arrived for my long-awaited appointment with Dr O'Loughlin. Full of excitement I was beaming when led into his office.

'Good morning Helen, how are you?'

'Hello doctor, I'm fine thank you.'

Hearing that serious tone I recognised all too well, and looking rather solemn, he said 'Helen I can't believe you could be pregnant, after all you've been through it would *really* be a miracle.'

'But Dr Leaney did a urine test followed by a blood test. He didn't believe it either so he did both,' I responded.

'That's good but Helen you *do* realise with your long history of gynaecological operations how impossible it would seem?'

'Yes I do but Dr O'Loughlin I *am* pregnant. I know I am. I know by the way I feel. I have no doubt. I did at first but now I *know* I am.'

'Well the tests have been done but unfortunately sometimes they can be wrong. Helen, I care about you, I don't want you to get your hopes up until we are certain beyond any doubt whatsoever. I'm not sure what it will do to you to discover the tests have been wrong. I can only pray now for your sake, by some miracle you are pregnant. It's been a long road. You've been through a great deal. So tell me, who is this man in your life?'

Although beginning to doubt Gary's sincerity I answered positively, 'Oh Dr O'Loughlin, Gary is really good to me and to Dani. We're very happy.'

'Well that's great news. I'm glad things are working out for you. I tell you what, instead of repeating the blood tests why don't we do an ultrasound? That way we'll both know right now, one way or the other.'

'You mean you can do an ultrasound now, right here? How things have changed since I was pregnant with Dani, and had to wait until I was seven months before you could send me to safely have an X-ray. Oh yes please let's do it *now*!'

'Ok I'll go and get the machine.'

Dr O'Loughlin wheeled in the ultrasound, and as I sat fascinated, he switched it on probably wondering why he was even bothering.

'Right let's do this,' he said.

Rolling the device gently across my pelvis we both silently watched the screen. I didn't know what I was looking at.

'Helen, if I didn't do this scan myself, I'd never have believed it.'

'What's wrong?' I asked impatiently.

'Do you see this little thing here?' he asked.

'What, that little squarish kind of shape that's flashing?'

'Yes Helen. That little squarish shape that's flashing is your baby's heartbeat. It should have been impossible for you to become pregnant. I don't know how but you most certainly *are* pregnant and your baby has a healthy strong heartbeat. It's an absolute miracle, and I am completely shocked. We'd better make some plans for you. Which hospital would you like to have your baby in?'

'I think perhaps I'd better not take any chances. I'd better go to the Queen Victoria Hospital, after all, it's the best hospital and I'd feel safe there in case anything goes wrong. I want my baby to have the best!'

'That's an excellent decision. We'll book you in straight away. I guess I'll see you again in a month. I don't have to tell you to look after yourself and your little miracle. Take care.'

'Thank you, I will and I'll see you soon.'

\*\*\*

As time progressed I began to feel more insecure. Gary was obviously stalling, and I had difficulty coming to terms with the unthinkable, admitting to myself the relationship I thought I had, wasn't to be. Denial was easier than to accept the inconceivable while seeing less and less of him. The bubble had burst with my world collapsing around me.

I couldn't grasp what had gone so wrong and tried in vain to encourage him to talk. I kept receiving the same response, 'I'll put it down to the fact you're pregnant and feeling a bit insecure. There's absolutely nothing wrong, everything's fine. I love you more than anything and nothing can ever change that, I just need more time to sort things out, that's all.'

All I could do was adopt a wait and see attitude. I was imagining there was a problem because I was pregnant. If there really was a problem, it was only a matter of time before it manifested.

My immediate concern was for the health and safety of Dani and my unborn child. Knowing enough to realise not to put any stress on a pregnancy, I made the decision that regardless of the outcome with Gary, I would manage on my own. I wouldn't dwell on broken dreams and what should have been.

He answered my calls but always with the same excuse. 'I'm sorry I can't talk now, I'm really busy.'

Nearing the end of the first trimester my intuition was telling me he wanted a way out. I didn't have any idea as to what had gone wrong, and all I asked was for the truth and a little respect. He tried to convince me our relationship was solid, and I was imagining problems because I was pregnant.

# *Royal Adelaide Hospital*

Gary left for Melbourne and it was the first time he didn't ring me while on an interstate business trip. I began making excuses for his absence as I couldn't accept what was happening.

While he was away I was in terrible pain and very frightened. I re-visited Dr Leaney who sent me straight to the Royal Adelaide Hospital (R.A.H.).

By the time I arrived in the Casualty Department I was positive the pain and pregnancy weren't related. The doctors assessing me were understandably limited as to what they could do because I was pregnant, so I underwent ultrasounds to no avail. It was my first introduction to the public health system and I hated it. Although it had been a constant financial struggle I always had private health cover but that day it meant nothing. I was in an old, depressing public hospital ward and the only difference between me and the person in the next bed was I would be billed.

Sharing a hectic, noisy room with at least a dozen old and frail patients all battling their own illnesses resulted in little or no sleep for anyone. Until that day I had only known hospitals with light and airy private rooms. I realised how valuable private health insurance was and made a mental note that regardless of how financially challenging life ever became, I would never give up my Private Health Fund membership.

It was 1987, fast approaching a new millennium, yet our public health system appeared to be in decline rather than advancing with many South Australian hospital buildings becoming dilapidated. The nursing staff, and level of care they provided, was exemplary. Medical teams stood at the foot of my bed discussing possible theories. I wanted to be involved in their conversations, for them to talk to me as I lay helpless on the bed.

I heard a variety of possible explanations for my pain; gallbladder, or perhaps it was kidney stones but the comment that distressed me the most, 'I think the baby is already dead.'

As they continued to speculate without involving me I couldn't help feel any more significant than the ground beneath them. The pain eased on the second day, and I began to regain an appetite. Asking for some food brought the response, 'you can't eat we may have to operate.' While I understood the statement, I also worried about how my baby would fare without nourishment for so long. I hadn't eaten for two days. I was nauseous and distraught, confused and angry.

They adopted the attitude to wait and see but the pain was easing, I was hungry, and if I didn't get some food my baby *would* die. I asked the nurses to ring Dr O'Loughlin to let him know I was there. He would arrange to have me transferred to the Queen Victoria Hospital where he would determine what the problem was, and remedy it. Believing my request had been enacted I awaited news of my transfer. I asked anyone who came near me to check and see if he'd been in contact because I couldn't fathom what was taking so long.

Assured he had been contacted but not responded, with nothing further done for me, I insisted on being discharged and returned to Dr Leaney. He declared the pain was most likely due to an ulcer which was feasible considering the stress I'd been under. After a great deal of reassurance the treatment wouldn't affect the pregnancy, I reluctantly agreed to take Mucaine and the pain soon disappeared, and never returned.

When I asked Dr O'Loughlin why he left me in the Royal Adelaide Hospital he looked surprised saying he was unaware of my plight, and no one had contacted him. I knew he wouldn't have let me down without good reason.

# *An abominable act*

By the fourth month of my pregnancy, my relationship with Gary was over, although he refused to admit it. Determined to find out what I'd done wrong I telephoned him, strongly suggesting he see me but still he continued with his pregnant and insecure excuses.

I told him he owed me and his unborn child the truth. I didn't care what it was, I only wanted honesty. He eventually visited stating his wife had been ill, and they thought she had cancer but the twins were fine.

Wife … cancer … twins. What twins? Whose twins? Speechless my mind went screeching into overdrive while my heart shattered.

How could I have been so stupid? I went into shock trying to comprehend the words coming out of his mouth. How did I get sucked into his web of deceit? He sat looking at me; eyes cold and lifeless. One of the reasons he said he was divorcing was because he'd apparently married a career person who he later discovered didn't want children. It was difficult for me to accept the reason we'd split was because his supposedly ex-wife was pregnant to him with twins! It was surely a bad dream that I would wake from, and everything would be fine.

Forced to come to terms with an eighteen month relationship based on lies, the days of living in denial were over. I had to accept after all that time, I was just an affair, and the fact I believed I couldn't have more children, evidently suited his plan perfectly. Until, the unthinkable happened. The next morning he rang to announce he wasn't coming back. 'But' he said, 'I'll be there when our baby is brought into this world.'

Bordering on panic, thoughts snowballing into trepidation, I had to take control of my life for Dani's sake, my baby, and my sanity. With support from family and friends I put the past where it belonged and reassessed our future. I believe everything happens for a reason so while I held that belief I looked forward to whatever fate had in store for us.

Dr O'Loughlin had said it was a miracle I'd conceived so there was a reason this baby was about to enter our world. I cannot put into words the frustration and confusion, the devastation I felt when Gary walked out on me, and his unborn child. He had been living two separate lives. Words can only go so far to describe such an abominable act.

Narrow-minded people pass judgement, without any comprehension of the tremendous soul-destroying experience such rejection creates, forcing a mother into single parenthood. Once I acknowledged our situation I began to feel relaxed and comforted by an intense consoling sensation I cannot describe. Healthy and unlike my pregnancy with Dani, over morning sickness within the first three months, I started to organise the nursery and every fortnight bought a baby item.

Dani's bassinette and a number of other essentials that had been passed around over the years were finding their way back to us. My Grandmother advised me in 1973, while awaiting the birth of Dani, to have a hospital bag packed by the time I reached seven months because, 'babies can be born any time after seven months you know.' Due on Labor Day, 8 October, Dani was born a week early. Lucky for me I had listened, so my bag was packed and ready to go.

***

In 1976 I had an ethereal dream when my grandmother appeared to me a week after she had passed away. I remember it as clearly as if it happened yesterday. The short version is that it was 11pm and I was awake. My grandmother was an atheist who didn't believe in anything religious, especially eternal life. In order to marry my father, my mother converted to Catholicism to enable them to hold their wedding service in a Catholic Church.

Shocked to see my grandmother knowing she had died I mumbled, 'It's Grandma,' and she responded with, 'Yes dear it's me, I'm here, I'm finally here, I am in no pain, I am in peace.' My grandfather, whom I adored, was a non-practising Catholic, and died seven years prior. He appeared at her side, smiled at me then they both faded out of sight.

The next day I fought an overwhelming urge to tell my mother, knowing it would upset her but I heard myself announce the news about my weird dream. Then I apologised.

As I expected she cried but surprised me when she exclaimed, 'that's my sign, oh God, that's my sign! Don't apologise, you were meant to tell me. No-one knows but I've been going to the church every morning praying for a sign that mum is at peace, and not in horrendous pain anymore. That wasn't a dream; you had a 'vision.' Mum has sent me the sign I've been begging for. Thank God I know now she's not in pain any more, she's at peace!'

As soon as my mother said I'd had a 'vision,' I realised she was right. If it was just a dream I would have been asleep but I was awake. I had heard of people experiencing 'visions' but never knew whether to believe it. From that moment I appreciated 'visions' are real and they *do* happen.

# Queen Victoria Hospital

Thursday, 9 July 1987, at twenty-eight week's gestation, life was coasting along relatively well. I had planned a lunch date with a girlfriend, Annette. Sitting at the kitchen table eating breakfast that morning, I suddenly felt damp. Deep in my soul I knew I was in trouble but rather than acknowledge the seriousness, I showered, changed and left for lunch.

As I locked the front door I heard a female voice whisper, 'Helen your water has broken.' I was taken aback as there wasn't anyone there but her words were direct and clear. I shook it off because I was pregnant and everyone knows weird things can happen during pregnancy. I was only six months, healthy, and never having experienced anything like it I considered, or should I say hoped, it was safe to ignore.

I kept reassuring myself it wasn't anything to worry about but while driving to Annette's house there was a sudden gush. Saturated, I was terrified. Trembling in fear barely able to see through tears I did a U-turn and headed home, fighting a losing battle with common sense, knowing I should've driven straight to hospital. Quivering I struggled to unlock the door, and once inside scarcely able to breathe, I stood with my back against it trying to come to terms with what was occurring.

With hands shaking, I managed to dial Dr O'Loughlin's phone number. Waiting for my call to be answered had a soothing effect. I was trusting he'd tell me everything would be fine, that I became alarmed unnecessarily and I would feel silly for getting myself into a distressed state. A voice interrupted the monotonous ringing tone, 'Dr O'Loughlin's surgery.'

'Hello Sue, its Helen Barr speaking, *please* I need to speak to Dr O'Loughlin.'

'I'm sorry he's with a patient.'

'It's ok, I'll wait.'

'He may be some time.'

'Please Sue, I think my water's broken. I'm only twenty eight weeks. I'll wait I need to speak to him.'

The response was immediate.

'One moment, I'll put you straight through.'

I managed to calm myself and gain an air of confidence. I was simply over-reacting.

'Hello Helen, how are you?'

Striving to remain composed, 'Oh Dr O'Loughlin I think I'm in trouble. I think my water's broken but it didn't happen with Dani, so I don't know whether it has or not. I'm frightened.'

There was silence apart from the sound of my heart pounding.

'Oh Helen you're only twenty-eight weeks. Get yourself straight to the Queen Victoria Hospital; if you're alone call an ambulance. I'll ring the hospital to tell them you're on your way and I'll meet you there.'

Accepting the seriousness, the concern in his voice evident, I was forced to face the inevitable. Before leaving for Annette's I left Dani in the care of my neighbours, and close friends Dianne, and her then husband Robert. Dani wanted to stay and play with their children instead of going out for lunch with me.

I phoned Dianne to let her know what was happening, and asked if she could look after Dani for the rest of the day, and I'd organise my mother to collect her later. Dianne insisted she'd be fine, not to worry, and Dani could stay as long as necessary.

Refusing to create a fuss I called my mother rather than an ambulance which proved to be a mistake as she was soon as panicked as I was. Waiting for her to arrive I phoned Annette to cancel lunch and she asked how far advanced my pregnancy was. When I replied I was barely into the twenty-eighth week she said the baby had a fighting chance. She definitely knew more about premature babies than I did. Turning my thoughts to Gary I considered ringing him but concluded if he cared about either of us, he wouldn't have left. Never had I felt so alone and petrified without any real perception of what to expect.

On arrival at the Queen Victoria Hospital we were immediately escorted into the High Dependency Unit. I quickly realised a premature birth can happen to anyone without warning for any reason but not knowing what to expect created apprehension and confusion I wasn't prepared for.

Dr O'Loughlin arrived looking worried. In all the years I'd known him I had never seen that expression on his face but I was immensely relieved knowing he was there for me.

Ordering an ultrasound to check how much fluid still surrounded the baby he said he hoped the worst scenario would be that I'd get bored bed-ridden in hospital for the next three months. If that were all it took for a healthy delivery I would happily become accustomed to living in hospital. He mentioned he was expected at a conference in Sydney, and had to board a plane but arranged for three of his colleagues to look after us until his return in two days.

Assuring him I'd be fine I told Dr O'Loughlin not to worry about us and settled down contemplating how to spend the days.

My mother left to collect Dani so she could come and see for herself that I was fine, and then she moved into my parent's home for the duration of my hospital stay. Dani was about to have her peaceful carefree existence torn to shreds. Throughout her life, family and friends closest to us had always referred to her as the perfect child, never causing a moment's grief.

My precious 'China Doll' had always been healthy, and a delight to raise, but now my innocent perfect child would be forced to grow up overnight. Our fun times all but ceased to exist, the life we shared swallowed up and lost forever in the nightmare about to consume us.

\*\*\*

Dr Sweet, the first of Dr O'Loughlin's colleagues enlisted to look after us arrived to check on our progress. I commented I thought it was all a big fuss about nothing and once Dr O'Loughlin returned, I'd probably be sent home. He said he doubted I'd be going anywhere and would be there for me should I need him through the night.

Later that evening with nothing else to do but think, realism was beginning to sink in. My baby could be born three months too soon, and I didn't know anything about a premature birth or what to expect from the baby.

I was ignorant and didn't know anyone I could talk to who had been through the same experience so I lay wondering how to quickly gain information. I yearned for someone to walk through the door and simply say, 'Hello I know what you're going through. I'm here if you need someone to talk to.'

Friday morning, Dr Mollison was the next colleague on the list. Ironically the last time I saw him was 30 September 1973, when he was called in to deliver Dani due to a misunderstanding. Hospital staff mistakenly thought Dr O'Loughlin had gone away for the weekend and called Dr Mollison in his absence.

Sitting on the end of the bed as though he had all day to spend comforting me, he explained what to expect from the birth but nothing about the effect on the baby. I had only been warned of the possibility of a slightly enlarged head, and a fine covering of hair over the baby's body. Thinking that was the worst to expect I tried not to worry about any dangers other than my baby could be born too soon, and would be very tiny. I reasoned that if the life of my baby were in serious jeopardy someone would warn me but still I couldn't relax.

Dr Mollison reassured me we'd be alright providing I didn't lose any more fluid, remained in bed, and didn't get an infection. Under strict instructions lying in hospital I laughed. How could I possibly get an infection? He left the room, and sometime later that day another gush, and anxiety with it. An ultrasound ordered urgently, revealed I had enough fluid left, and there wasn't any immediate danger.

Until midnight Friday 10 July I was the only patient in a share room in the High Dependency Ward. A nursing sister entered to advise me an emergency patient from the Modbury Hospital had arrived and would be sharing the room. The curtain drawn I couldn't see the lady but it was evident she was in more trouble than I was. Even though the care I received was exceptionally friendly and commendable, that room was a frightening place to be, and by then I was sobbing uncontrollably, completely disillusioned, and absolutely terrified.

The new patient threatening to give birth at twenty-six weeks made me concede things weren't as bad for us as I thought. I couldn't help overhear her doctor saying if her baby weighed at least one kilogram there was a chance to save it. Experiencing heavy contractions her doctors were desperate to control them. They could hear me crying and I heard her husband ask, 'Where the hell is that poor girl's husband she shouldn't be going through this on her own.'

Their time expired and they were rushed into theatre. I didn't see them with the curtain drawn but my heart went with them as I deliberated if their baby could survive at twenty-six weeks, then mine at twenty-eight weeks had a fantastic chance. Recognising the harsh reality we would be next, my thoughts turned to people in prison cells on death row. I could relate to how they felt. You know it's inevitable but don't know when it's actually going to happen.

Eager to know the fate of my room-mate I kept asking whoever walked through the door if they could find out how they were but either they didn't know or wouldn't tell me. I was compelled to presume they sadly lost their fight. If only I had been taken on a tour through the Neo-Natal Intensive Care unit, and shown the fragile babies born as early as twenty-four weeks and thriving, I would have been spared a great deal of angst while in High Dependency. To have been shown that tiny babies really do have a chance, would have helped me enormously. After all, I was only going into hospital as a precaution.

Saturday, 11 July 1987, at 9am Dr McCusker was on duty looking after us. I hadn't met him before but he was exhibiting all the traits I had come to expect from Dr O'Loughlin's colleagues.

'I'm only showing you a face to go with the name, and I'll be here for you today if you need me but I'm not expecting any dramas, and Dr O'Loughlin will be returning tonight.'

Confident nothing would change I told him to enjoy his Saturday because we wouldn't need him. I mentioned I was bored, and wanted something to do if I was to be stuck in that room for three months.

He laughed and suggested I make the most of it because soon enough I would be wishing I could rest. He had only just left the room when there was another gush of fluid. As a chill shivered down my spine, clutching the call button I summoned a nurse.

Traumatised, I managed to tell her I had lost the remaining fluid. The look on the poor girl's face was one of horror; a look that said *why* on her shift. I've never seen anyone move so fast as she rushed off to page Dr McCusker. He would have still been in the hospital but didn't reply. I think every staff member passed through my room all desperate to help in some way.

# *The whisper*

The ward thrown into pandemonium, nursing sisters were running in and out of my room awaiting his return. The hours passed with Dr McCusker oblivious to the duress unfolding as our condition deteriorated rapidly. Staff members continued to page him, at a loss as to why he wasn't responding. Spiking a raging temperature I was throwing off blankets one minute, the next begging for more. I couldn't stop shaking as a queer indescribable state of consciousness swathed my body.

Drained and weary I felt like I was floating on air, somehow aware that if I were to succumb to the sensation we would die. Fighting the urge to sleep I kept reporting each symptom as instructed, with every ounce of strength I could muster to stay awake. A wide black belt attached to a machine was wrapped firmly around me to monitor the baby, and a button placed in my hand to press every time I felt a movement. I was then left alone, and it was at that moment I realised I hadn't felt anything for a while. The situation had become extremely dangerous with slim chance of a safe delivery.

At approximately 2pm Dr McCusker rushed into the room breathless. There had been a problem with his pager and he had no idea we were in trouble, and couldn't apologise enough. He sat on the bed explaining the infection he warned me of earlier but this time it had a name, Group B Strep. I had heard of it but had no idea what it was or what it meant to us. Although he had swabs taken from me to confirm his diagnosis of the infection, all results returned negative.

Many years of experience convinced him, regardless of the outcome technology returned, I indeed had this Group B Strep which lies dormant in a large percentage of women, and generally doesn't have any consequence. It is a common organism like any other with the exception, should it flare up during childbirth, apparently it can be fatal to both mother and baby.

Dr McCusker said my symptoms were confusing but because every patient is different, each must be treated accordingly, so in his wisdom ignored the negative swabs.

'Helen if I'm wrong, I'm sorry but I don't know what else it can be and what more I can do for you but I have to try. There aren't any guarantees. I'm losing both of you and fast running out of time.' Critically ill *our* time had expired, and my baby must be born without further delay.

'Helen I need you to make a decision only you can make. I need to know whether you want me to do an emergency caesarean or whether you prefer for nature to take its course, and deliver naturally.'

I asked how much time we had.

'We don't have any more time. If I'm to do a caesarean I must act immediately.'

Vital seconds ticking away, the following exchange took place rapidly with profound urgency in both voices.

'Doctor if I decide to have it naturally what can I expect?'

'You'll eventually go into labour but how long that will take I can't be sure,' he replied.

'What chance will my baby have if I go down that road?'

'None whatsoever Helen. Your baby won't survive a natural birth. You'll be delivering a dead baby.'

Choking on tears I managed, 'Caesarean.'

'Ok, let's go.' Dr McCusker turned and signalled to the group who had quietly gathered in my room. Within a split second a full-scale mission swung into action with no less than precision movement. Dr McCusker then turned back to me. 'Helen there's one more decision I need you to make. If things don't go well in there I need to know whose life you want me to save, if it comes to that. We don't have much time I have to act now.'

That moment will be imprinted in my memory forever with sheer dread. Never in my entire life had I known such loneliness and deep sorrow. How could I make that decision? How could anyone. I needed time to think but there wasn't any time left. What would the ramifications of *any* decision be? Categorically shocked and broken, either I die to save my baby, or I live and lose the baby. Why did *I* have to decide? I'm not God so let Him decide. That's it! Let *Him* decide.

Looking into the doctor's eyes I strained to find the words.

'Helen I need your answer now. We've run out of time.'

'Dr McCusker, please I want my baby to be given every possible chance.'

I had to trust in my frazzled faith as I put our lives in his hands. From that day forward, and over many years to come I resisted making the simplest of decisions. Staying with my parents while Chiara was in hospital, if my mother simply asked me what I wanted for tea, I became upset and frustrated. I didn't care if I went hungry I just didn't want to have to make *any* decisions at all. All and any questions from anyone were answered with, 'I don't care.'

# *The birth*

As the orderly was readying my bed to wheel me off to the operating theatre, I heard a female whisper once again. 'Trust in God Helen, just Trust in God.' Turning my head to see who the lady was, there wasn't anyone there so I must have imagined it. Just as I did when I heard the words, 'your water has broken.'

While everyone was rushing around preparing me for theatre I thought of Dani and my family. I didn't have the chance to say goodbye to any of them, and I wanted to see Dani to hold her and tell her how much I loved her. I longed to see my family one last time. I hadn't gone through the affect Gary's desertion had; although I despised him I needed him. I was desperately lonely believing my baby and I would die.

As we reached the theatre doors the procession came to an abrupt halt. A nurse was waving a telephone and I presumed it must've been an urgent call for the doctor but it was for me. The staff were anxious I take the call because I had insisted no-one be told of our plight. The staff didn't agree with my decision, so if I took the call then at least someone would know what was happening to us.

The telephone was put to my ear and it was my friend and business partner Judy. The procession moved off with me blubbering into the telephone. Judy had no idea of her timing.

Crying into the phone I told her we weren't expected to live but not to tell my family until it was all over, and then to let Gary know.

Judy thought better of it, and although my parents were out visiting relatives at the time, she rang around until she found them, and then tracked down Gary who casually replied, 'Thank you Judy,' and hung up. She then travelled to the hospital to join my family.

Lifted onto the operating table I wondered why we needed so many people, and was informed most of them were there for my baby. Snivelling uncontrollably with fear, I again heard the mysterious whisper repeating the words, 'Trust in God Helen, just Trust in God,' as I surrendered to the anaesthetic.

Opening my eyes all I could see was white. Everywhere I looked was white, and in a daze I noticed the sea of faces had disappeared. Alone and frightened I couldn't move. Scanning the room I wondered where I was. Was I dead or alive? It was very quiet and I couldn't see anyone so I thought I must have died. Was I in Heaven or Hell? It couldn't be Hell because everything was white, and it was too cold so I must've made it to Heaven. Heaven would be white.

Bordering on hysteria I wanted to scream, 'Where's my baby' but I was too terrified to hear the words that my baby had died. Then it occurred to me the staff must've thought I died too, and put me in the morgue. As the anaesthetic started wearing off I realised I survived, and wasn't dead at all but I couldn't move. The last thing I remembered was being rushed into theatre, and people running in all directions. The entire scenario had been one of frenzy in a desperate fight for life, and the sombre atmosphere that existed had vanished.

There wasn't a sound or movement. It was the weirdest sensation I had ever experienced, apart from when I felt like I was floating above my bed earlier that morning. I can't explain what it was like to wake up numb without any feeling in my body, and all I could see was white. I assumed the worst until I heard a whisper but that time it was a male voice. 'Do you know what you've had?'

I turned slightly expecting no-one to be there but I was gazing into a beautiful warm pair of eyes. Heart thumping I simply replied, 'No, I don't.'

The whisper continued, 'You have a beautiful little girl, and she's all arms and legs.'

Presuming he had made a mistake, and convinced I gave birth to a boy who hadn't survived I replied, 'No I had a boy.' I expected him to apologise but he looked at me and smiled.

I'm sure he thought I was crazy. 'Oh no, you most certainly *do* have a little girl.'

I dearly wanted another daughter and worried how I would raise a son supposing it's probably easier for a single mother to raise a daughter than a son. Not believing I gave birth to a girl I was wheeled bed and all into the Neo-Natal Intensive Care Unit. I had never heard of the unit, so beyond that door was a world of which I had no knowledge.

Apart from the continual beeping of a variety of monitors, barely a sound could be heard, and yet there were many people all quietly going about the business of saving 'their' baby. The atmosphere in the unit is difficult to describe. Sterile, yet peaceful. Solemn, yet friendly. Serious, yet smiling. They were a breed of people I didn't know existed. Angels on earth, on an incredible mission to save the tiniest babies. The only equipment I recognised were the humidi-cribs and I later learned a humidi-crib was often a positive sign.

Walking through the unit filled my soul with awe. We stopped alongside a strange looking contraption at waist height resembling a flat open transparent box with mechanical devices attached above and below it. Here I was introduced to my tiny fragile baby. Lying in the shallow box she was attached to numerous wires, tubes, drips, and a ventilator that was taped to her face. The crib was about two feet (approximately 61cms) square surrounded by a border of clear Perspex approximately three inches in height and covered with plastic film, under which my baby lay.

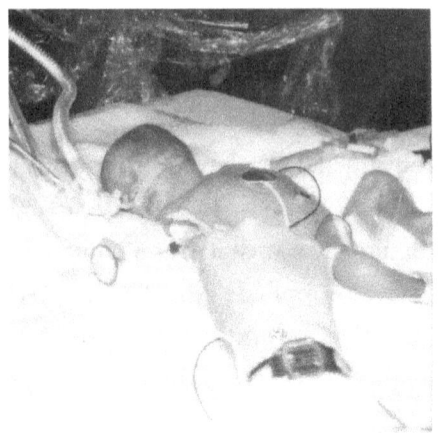

*Chiara one day old…not much bigger than my fist*

I had only known plastic film to be used for keeping food fresh. It was explained the plastic not only kept in warmth but also allowed quick access in an emergency, access which cannot be gained fast enough in a humidi-crib. Overhead there was a canopy with an inbuilt heater, and to the side on the shelf were monitors of different shapes and sizes, all playing a vital role in keeping my baby alive.

Due to having jaundice, a special type of light was used to treat it. Whenever she was turned facing the light, a tiny pair of 'sunglasses' were placed over her eyes to avoid any damage to them. Tears again welling, an inner peace mixed with trepidation filtered through me. I was too frightened to bond too closely, afraid of losing her. The more I love her, the more it will hurt if I lose her.

# *Neo-Natal Intensive Care Unit*

Riding a roller coaster of emotions I wondered how Chiara could possibly survive. Noticing a priest standing next to her my heart sank but then I remembered asking the nurses to contact Father Farmer from St Ignatius Church Norwood to baptise her the moment she was born. Overcome with emotion I hadn't grasped the fact I had a baby girl, and it wasn't until I heard Fr Farmer ask someone what *her* name was, I accepted I really *did* have another daughter.

As I looked up at Fr Farmer to see who he was talking to, I noticed my mother and brother Trevor, standing next to him. When he received the news we were in trouble, he boarded the first plane out of Melbourne. Trevor immediately agreed to be Godfather, and the baptism was conducted in the sterile, serene surrounds of the Neo-Natal Intensive Care Unit of the Queen Victoria Hospital.

My perfect tiny baby, born twelve weeks prematurely was baptised, and proudly named Chiara Jo. Believing all through my pregnancy I was having a boy, I thought I would be naming him Cameron, and he would bear the name John as a middle name and tribute to my gynaecologist John O'Loughlin. After all, if it wasn't for him this baby wouldn't have been possible. I couldn't name a girl John, so I took his initials JO, and seriously considered extending it to Joanna but then thought Chiara Joanna would have been a bit much.

Weighing in at 1030 grams or about two pounds, she measured fourteen inches or approximately thirty-six centimetres in length. Her head measured ten centimetres in circumference and was not grossly out of proportion to her body, as I had been warned to expect. Her skin was transparent. Her ears resembling dried apricots were still forming, and she had a 'film' where her nails developed over the next three months. Fingers no wider than matchsticks were about half the length of one.

The palms of her hands measured less than two centimetres, approximately one inch, and her feet approximately half-an-inch, or one centimetre wide, and one-and-a-half inches, or about three centimetres, in length. Her eyelashes were barely visible, and she didn't have eyebrows. Her gums had a gap in them that later closed. Covered in fine fair hair, her tiny body was approximately three inches, or six centimetres, in width.

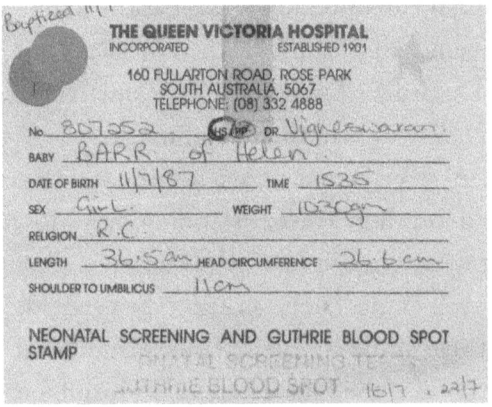

*Chiara's details attached to her crib*

I remarked how healthy she looked, even with all the drips, drains and tubes attached, and wondered how they found her tiny veins. Chiara had been administered a drug to paralyse her body for the first few days so she couldn't fight against the ventilator. Seeing her lying there so peaceful I could see she wasn't in pain, and believing the worst was over I thought all she had to do was to grow and come home. I was wrong.

Gravely ill without chance of survival, nothing could have prepared me for what I was about to hear when Dr Vigneswaran entered the room. An extraordinary paediatrician, he tenderly explained that the Group B Strep had poisoned my fluid, and because Chiara had swallowed a small amount during the traumatic birth, it resulted in her being born with septicaemia (commonly referred to as blood poisoning). Dr Vigneswaran believed she was too ill to survive, and gave her one hour at best.

Unable to feed, a nasal gastric tube was inserted, and also taped to her face. My baby was dying, and there wasn't anything further anyone could do to help, leaving me despairing for better news. The nursing sister assigned to her, regularly applied physiotherapy by patting Chiara's chest with two fingers, and each session finished with putting a tube through the nostril, and down into her lungs to suction out the excess fluid, an essential element of the life-saving regime.

Tears rolling down my cheeks, I begged God to let my baby live, and again I heard the lady whisper, 'Trust in God Helen, just trust in God.'

I wondered where that voice was coming from. Chiara survived the first hour much to the amazement of everyone in the Intensive Care Unit, in particular Dr Vigneswaran, who by that time, we were told to refer to, as Dr Viggy.

Second by second we made it through the twenty-four hour mark as a cautious sigh of relief swept through the unit. No one expected such a courageous fight; there wasn't any doubt she was a little battler. A photograph taken by one of the nurses took pride of place next to my bed.

Dr Viggy, a highly proficient, compassionate soul who ensured his precious babies were given his undivided care and attention, came to tell me if she could survive the next twenty-four hours, she might have a chance. When Chiara remained stable through that critical period there was a distinct wave of relief but she was still in danger, with a long journey ahead. Paralysed, unable to walk since giving birth, I was frustrated at losing my independence. I had to rely on staff and a wheelchair to take me down to Intensive Care to see Chiara.

Early on Sunday morning while most people were sleeping in, Dr O'Loughlin walked into the room disappointed and apologising for not attending the birth, especially as he hadn't been there when Dani was born either. We shared a joke saying someday the pair of us would get our acts together. He then reassured me he would have proceeded in exactly the same manner as Dr McCusker. I had confidence in all decisions Dr McCusker made but was relieved to have Dr O'Loughlin back. When I told him I couldn't walk he promised it was just nature's way of ensuring I had some rest.

As soon as staff said Chiara could have visitors I met Dani and my parents in my room. They then pushed me in the wheelchair down to see her. As I placed a finger on the bell of the glass door in order to gain entry to the Intensive Care Unit, I could see partitions had been drawn around Chiara's crib. I had seen those partitions around other cribs so I was aware it often meant tragedy, and burst into tears. My family stood baffled not knowing what was wrong, and I couldn't tell them.

David, who I recognised as looking after Chiara the day before, could see I was distressed and came to the door ushering us into the side room to explain what had happened. I was convinced I had 'lost' her, until he said 'Chiara has developed what we term severe lung disease, meaning her lung has leaked. A tube has to be inserted into it to drain the fluid.' The news upset me but at least she was alive. Wiping away tears I tried to comprehend what was said but all I heard after that was, 'as soon as the doctors are finished I'll come back out and get you.'

It's common for a premature baby to suffer lung problems due to their immaturity. Knowing the problem could be dealt with helped ease the anxiety but not the helplessness. I wanted to be with my baby so she would know I was there, and show her I had brought Dani and my parents to visit.

Eventually permitted inside, the first thing I noticed on approaching her crib was a note stating 'No more heel pricks.' Bruises were a direct result of blood samples taken from her heels. The note disappeared a couple of days later, and then reappeared at regular intervals. Positioning my wheelchair as close to the crib as possible we noticed the tube inserted into her lung, and as hard as it was to look at, it was there to save her life.

Every second was regarded a bonus, and it was difficult leaving and returning to my room but for as much as I didn't want to go, I had to try to look after myself. We were in for a lengthy stay so I had to be sensible and try to eat and sleep. I became obsessed and couldn't bear to think of her alone and crying, so I set a pattern hoping she would tune in to, that would help me too. In the mornings I waited at the unit door for the doctors to finish their rounds. I remained with her between meals, and stayed until late at night.

As a single mother practically living in the Neo-Natal Intensive Care Unit I was approached at different times by parents all asking the same question, 'How do you manage to deal with all this stress on your own?' My response simple, 'Because I have to.'

The truth was I convinced myself it was easier without a husband around. I watched couples come and go, and initially the fathers generally would be in the unit as much as the mothers, arriving together and leaving together.

As time progressed, I witnessed the presence of the fathers dwindle, presumably and understandably due to work commitments. I looked at other mothers sitting with their babies, and felt better off than them not having to clock watch to go home and cook tea or iron shirts.

I had been working casual hours but with Chiara so ill, and wanting to be at her side every day, I resigned and relied solely on Centrelink payments with my employer stating I could return at any time. Money was tight but I didn't care because I was with my baby. I had the freedom to come and go as I pleased, and some mothers with unsupportive husbands were envious, telling me I was lucky to be on my own but by then I already knew that. Dani was my only real concern outside the hospital walls, and she was well cared for by my parents. Thankfully I didn't have to worry about her.

I commented to a nurse that my baby looked healthy even though she wasn't but instead of agreeing with me, she showed me another baby who looked terribly emaciated and said Chiara should look the same. What I wrongly assumed was a healthy look, was in fact the swollen effect of the septicaemia.

My baby was bloated as a result of the blood poisoning, while the healthier baby had ribs showing, bones draped with skin, and this was how Chiara should look. It came as a tremendous shock but once Dr Viggy cured the septicaemia Chiara too would adopt the healthier look. All that could be done had been, and with her survival marked in seconds, daily life became a waiting game.

The best I could do, was try to keep up my milk supply which was fed into Chiara via a nasal gastric tube, with her first feed measuring a mere two milligrams. A course of Maxalon was prescribed for me as it had been found that it not only helped nausea but also aided milk supply. I continued the regime until we went home, however my supply soon diminished forcing me to admit defeat. Stroking and talking to her was often interrupted by alarms, and although I became accustomed to the different sounds I couldn't get used to what they meant knowing any one of them could sound disaster.

Episodes of her heart rate dropping were known as bradycardias, and she also suffered numerous apnoeas where she stopped breathing, sounding an alarm. Watching how the staff responded each time, I was able to mimic their actions and stimulate her by smacking gently on her bottom or lightly knocking on the crib and it was comforting knowing I could actually do something to help my baby.

I thought I was familiar with all the alarms but one sounded I hadn't heard before. 'It's ok Helen it's only the alarm to tell me the blood transfusion is finished.'

'She had a blood transfusion?'

'Helen she'll need many transfusions before she's healthy enough to leave here.' Chiara received blood from strangers, people who had taken valuable time out of their busy schedules to donate so my baby and others could live. Blood was often taken from me for cross

## Neo-Natal Intensive Care Unit 43

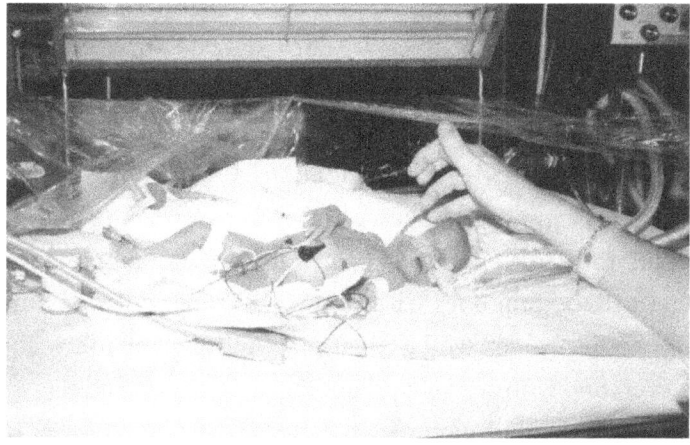

*All I could do was stroke her but with her ribs showing she was beginning to take on a healthier look*

matching but I was never given a reason why she couldn't be transfused with *my* blood – considering I was her mother and we share the same blood group – yet I can donate to others.

A new mother would expect her first cuddle within seconds but all I could do was wait patiently holding a tiny hand or foot, whichever didn't have a drip in it. As hard as it was, I was happy just to be with her as she lay under the plastic film. I developed an obsession taking photos craving all the memories I could get, aware I could lose her at any moment.

Too tiny to wear nappies she lay on top of the smallest available disposable nappy, and I looked forward to the day I could put her *in* one. Bearing too many drips and drains, and too tiny to wear clothes that would only be in the way of all the tubes, the overhead heater attached to her crib kept her warm. Eventually she grew into dolls clothes but I had to wait for her to grow enough to wear all the new clothes I had bought for a full-term baby.

When my close friend Julie visited she couldn't believe how tiny Chiara was, and when she returned approximately a week later, handed me the tiniest cardigan I had ever seen that her mother kindly knitted. It fitted on the palm of my hand but was too big so she had to grow into it.

As cards and flowers began to arrive, I felt guilty knowing what we needed most was money to enable the hospital to buy essential equipment, so very sick babies wouldn't have to share monitors etc. Not wishing to offend anyone Chiara's birth notice went in the paper with a request for donations to the Neo-Natal Intensive Care Unit in lieu of flowers and cards. It had the desired effect and I was happier knowing a few extra dollars found their way towards the unit.

Reading the cards I realised appropriate ones for a premature birth didn't exist. Receiving ones with the word 'Congratulations' and pictures of healthy babies while Chiara lay fighting for life was taxing. Nearly everyone who sent a card apologised for not finding one with appropriate wording or picture.

I contacted Judy to tell her I couldn't focus on our dream as Chiara was too ill for me to concentrate on anything else. We donated the dolls to the hospital to help raise more funds. The grant we received was mercifully written off, for which I was exceptionally grateful.

# *Only a miracle can save her*

Placed in an empty share room on the maternity ward, I was relieved to have the solitude to deal with my grief. The understanding was, no-one else would be put into the room, and I would be allocated a private room as soon as one became available. Chiara was less than two days old when my peaceful domain was shattered by staff busily moving objects.

I presumed the items were required elsewhere but then a smiling woman was wheeled in on a bed with an entourage of stuffed toys, balloons and noisy inconsiderate visitors. The woman had given birth to a healthy boy. The champagne and flowers followed as the room continued to fill with congratulations and excitement. It wasn't her fault, she couldn't have known what happened but I became agitated craving my own baby's survival. I knew it was selfish but I wanted to be left in private, not share in someone else's celebrations.

Dr Viggy appeared in the doorway looking troubled. Over the noise and laughter of my neighbour and her visitors, he explained Chiara had suffered a Grade 3 brain haemorrhage. (They are graded 1, 2, 3 or 4, depending on the severity with a '4' being the worst). He didn't expect her to survive considering she was also battling the septicaemia, and severe lung disease. He warned me that I could lose her at any second. He then left me alone to come to terms with the latest heart-breaking development.

I could hear his softly spoken voice in the corridor reprimanding someone for being so insensitive and forcing me into an unfair position of having to share the room with a mother of a healthy newborn. He ordered I be moved, and within minutes, I was in a private room. My life was out of control and I had great difficulty understanding what was unfolding around me. Utterly destroyed, again I heard the mysterious whisper repeating the words, 'Trust in God Helen, trust in God' but as usual there wasn't anyone there.

Beginning to think I was going insane I wondered who the voice belonged to and why she kept whispering to me. If she was real I should be able to see her. I didn't tell anyone about the whispering woman because no-one would have believed it.

The birth of a baby is supposed to be a celebratory time, yet I was a traumatised wreck. I had never considered the possibility of a premature birth. Things like that only happen to other people. Healthy women have healthy full-term babies, or so I thought. I held fears for a stillbirth or deformity but it had only ever been a thought not a reality.

Still reeling from the news of Chiara's brain haemorrhage, I heard Dr O'Loughlin's voice as he and a nurse approached. He had arrived to pay his morning visit, as he did every day to check on our progress. Looking uneasy, his greeting followed with, 'Helen is your baby covered by private health insurance?' A sense of panic washed through me. What else could be thrown at me, how much more could I take?

I was a private patient but my baby wasn't covered. I couldn't give her the best medical care. How could I raise a substantial amount of money to pay for Dr Viggy's services? An ominous feeling of desolation overwhelmed me as I asked, 'Dr O'Loughlin, no she isn't covered. What am I going to do?'

Gary had promised to organise a family health benefit and I hadn't given it another thought. I presumed we would *both* be insured by the time the baby was due.

I nominated Dr Vigneswaran as our paediatrician when I booked in to the hospital, as every person who knew him assured me he was the best, and that was a good enough recommendation for me.

Dr O'Loughlin simply said, 'Don't worry.' He would have a meeting with Dr Viggy and explain our circumstances. I was grossly ashamed at not having the money, or insurance cover, to save my baby.

Dr Viggy, presuming Chiara was a private patient, had automatically taken charge of her care. I was placed in a disturbing dilemma, not knowing how I could ever pay him for his services, and it had only been two days.

Inconsolable, grieving for what should have been, it was all too much to bear when Dr Viggy re-appeared. Staring into his eyes, too weak and embarrassed to speak, I was expecting he had come to tell me as Chiara was a public patient, he would have to dismiss himself and hand her over to the hospital.

'… Permission … Chiara …'

In a haze I could hear him speak but I wasn't listening, then I realised he had stopped talking.

Looking at me with his beautiful big brown eyes he continued.

'Helen are you alright? Did you hear what I just asked you?' I wanted to thank him for what he did for my baby and pledge to find the money to pay him.

He looked concerned. 'Helen I want to ask *your permission* to continue looking after Chiara. Dr O'Loughlin has explained your circumstances and I'd like to keep treating her as my patient, if you will agree. You won't be billed.'

Dr Viggy was standing at my bedside asking my permission! Tears made way for a smile from ear to ear. Overwhelmed by his generosity, I was beyond ecstatic at having Dr Viggy and the best team and technology available to help my baby thrive.

He and this team of special angels in the Neo-Natal Intensive Care Unit had every reason to believe Chiara wouldn't survive, and yet they continued to fight along with her.

Every second of every day, a pair of expert eyes were on her. No-one was prepared to give up. Conceived against all the odds, her quality of life questionable, the devoted team worked tirelessly around the clock attending to her every need.

The part of her brain that haemorrhaged is apparently known as the 'dark side.' I was warned she could have Cerebral Palsy, would probably never walk, and most likely suffer seizures. She would also grapple with mathematics, due to the area of the brain that had been affected. I deemed it a waste of vital energy to dwell on what may or may not be.

Dr Viggy returned. 'I'm so sorry Helen, things aren't good.'

Horrified I didn't want him to say any more but the awkward silence was soon broken.

'I don't know how to tell you this but, only a miracle can save Chiara now. We've done all we can, it's now only a matter of time. I want you to be prepared, because there's nothing more we can do.'

How could any parent prepare for the imminent loss of their child? My heart felt as though it had been ripped from my body, my brain was mush, my soul traumatised. All things medically possible had been achieved, and although we had massive support, we were on our own. Having nothing more than medications, monitors, machines, drips, drains and watchful eyes, staff did their best to ensure she was as comfortable as possible.

Each second that passed was a second in our favour. Could she find enough strength to battle through and eventually come home? It was a very frightening time but where there's life, there's hope. I refused to give up. Holding Chiara's delicate hand, I reflected on the words I so often heard whispered, and resolved to trust in God; it was all I had left to cling to.

# *Chiara's rainbow*

By the third day, Chiara's life faltering, her strength and determination had already touched many hearts. It seemed everyone was praying, and even people we didn't know were sending messages of support while offering prayers for a miracle. I was one of four children born to Catholic parents, who raised us to have faith and believe in eternal life. We were taught prayers I never understood, and simply recited parrot-fashion in school and in church as directed.

Every Sunday as we were growing up, our parents ensured we attended St Ignatius Church in Norwood. By the time I was 16-years-old, employed with a driver's licence, and bored with long-winded, too often repeated, sermons and prayers, I stopped attending. I was no longer a church-going Catholic but I had developed strong beliefs that I continued to garner strength from daily.

With Chiara so ill I had begun to appreciate the value of that faith, it was helping me through the most horrendous experience of my life. It caused me to contemplate how people without any religious faith, cope in a crisis.

Lying awake all night pleading for a miracle, I did my best to recall words to prayers I didn't understand. I asked my sister Teresa, who the

Patron Saint for sick mothers and children was. She reminded me, Saint Gerard.

I started praying to Saint Jude, Patron Saint of hopeless cases and to Saint Gerard for my baby, and the strength I craved. Beseeching all the help I could gather, I believed if a miracle weren't granted that night it never would be. To suffer the loss of a child would have me lose whatever was left of my sanity, so I frantically prayed for a sign, seeking proof beyond doubt that my baby would live.

Endeavouring to prepare myself for the worst, my thoughts returned to Dani. We were a team. It was Dani who displayed all the confidence but it worried me how she'd manage if the worst should prevail, as she was the least prepared. Remembering my mother had once begged for a sign and received it, I decided to try it myself and pleaded all night for a sign I could recognise to tell me Chiara would survive.

Dawn was breaking, so too was I, and it was raining heavily. Was that my sign? A sign of sadness; tears from Heaven? Depressed and expecting to hear Chiara had deteriorated I rang the Intensive Care Unit from my bed to be told there hadn't been any improvement but she was stable. As soon as the nurse arrived with a wheelchair I was taken down to see her. Peeling the plastic film back that was covering her crib, I sat holding her hand. It was all I was able to do. Sometimes she appeared to be crying but there wasn't a sound to be heard.

I arranged for my mother and Dani to visit later that day. Back in my room while awaiting their arrival, I was gazing out of the window and noticed the rain had stopped. There before my eyes appeared the widest, brightest rainbow I had ever seen. One end was on a tree outside my window, stretching over the hospital building towards the hills in the east. I stood in awe as I recalled learning in primary school that a rainbow was God's promise to Noah that he and his animals would be spared. All of a sudden I realised *that* rainbow was *my* sign! It was God's promise to me that Chiara would be spared. She would survive!

Sensing the unmistakable calming presence of God Himself, St Gerard and the hand of St Jude felt gently on my shoulder, our prayers had not only been heard they had been answered. I recall thinking, perhaps I wasn't such a flawed Catholic afterall. Dani arrived to find me again in tears and all I could do was point to the rainbow. Perplexed she asked what was wrong. Through my tears I told her I had prayed for a sign, and reminded her of the meaning of the rainbow. She candidly replied, 'Mum, I keep telling you she'll be alright. I *know* she will.'

Before Dani had a chance to say anything further, my mother came rushing into the room beaming with excitement. She was raving about the most beautiful rainbow she had ever seen, telling me the end of it was in their front garden, in the foothills, five suburbs away. Guiding her over to the window she was stunned to see the other end on the tree near my room. We all cried tears of joy.

Bursting with confidence we went down to the unit and rang the doorbell. I shall never forget the look on Sister Jan Ramsay's face as she greeted us, sporting a huge smile and an air of optimism.

'She's improved Helen, I don't know how but she's improved!'

Never will I forget that moment. We had been granted a miracle! There was absolutely no doubt about it and no other explanation. Chiara *would* survive.

# *First cuddle*

Our celebrations were short lived. Arriving at the door of Intensive Care on the morning of the fourth day I noticed a partition once again set up. Seeing people quickly moving about startled me. I had no idea what was taking place behind that curtain. I again thought I 'lost' her, when a few minutes later someone appeared at the door and escorted me into the side room. I was beginning to hate that room. Trembling with fear I could barely breathe.

It was explained to me that Chiara's other lung had leaked and it too required a drain. That news came as a semi-relief as I understood what to expect, since it had happened previously.

The lung problem repeated a third and final time resulting in another drain and another scar to add to her growing collection.

One morning, as I was sitting beside Chiara's crib, a team of doctors, specialists and therapists arrived, headed by Dr Haslam who introduced himself and the group to me. Numerous people were working behind the scenes ensuring each and every baby was afforded the best chance of survival. Dr Haslam was an integral, much appreciated member of our team who also worked relentlessly to save Chiara.

On the fifth day I recognised a man I had known through work, sitting with a woman beside a nearby crib. I was astonished to discover they were the same two people who arrived from the Modbury Hospital and shared my room that second horrific night in the High Dependency Unit. Their baby, although born at only twenty-six weeks, not only survived but was healthy. Chiara had been exceedingly unlucky. Anything that could happen to a premature baby happened to her, while baby Ryan sailed through unscathed.

I questioned Dr Viggy and Dr O'Loughlin as to why Chiara was born so prematurely considering I had been healthier physically than I had for a long time. Both doctors returned the same answer. They had tried to find a medical reason but failed. I learned then that the impact stress can have on the body is under-estimated. In their expert opinions, the only factor to play a part was festering stress. I hadn't dealt with Gary's departure and because of that my pregnancy became a time bomb. Hearing their explanation made me angry. Was it all Gary's fault? My baby, *his* baby was dying and he didn't care.

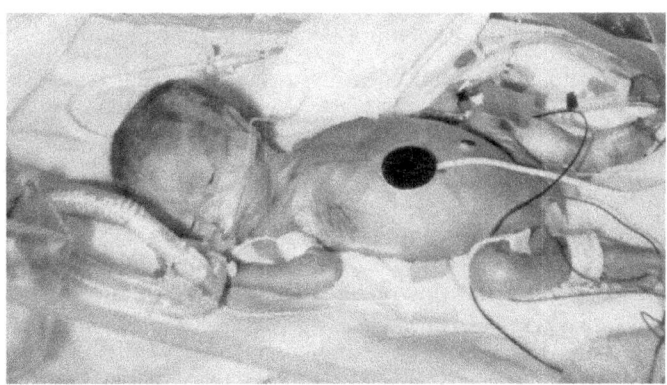

*Chiara with her scar from the drain in her lung*

\*\*\*

As the days slowly passed the septicaemia subsided and the lung disease settled. Nine days later staff were too busy to take me in a wheelchair to visit Chiara which made me determined to get there on my own. I managed to stagger down to the unit by holding the railing along the walls and arrived exhausted. The staff insisted I should have called them and they would have come to collect me themselves. I told them they had far more important things to do.

On the tenth day, as a direct result of the brain haemorrhage, Chiara's head began to swell. It became an oval shape due to the pressure of fluid in her brain building up, rounding off her fontanel or 'soft spot' as it is more commonly referred to. Discussions were held and the decision made to call in Mr Hanieh, a neurosurgeon from the Adelaide Children's Hospital.

Mr Hanieh arrived. He took just a few minutes to ascertain a shunt would have to be inserted to drain the excess cerebrospinal fluid from Chiara's brain. I was distraught to learn the haemorrhage had caused a condition known as hydrocephalus or 'water on the brain.' My baby would have to undergo neurosurgery (brain surgery). If left untreated it could cause head enlargement and compression of the brain.

There are four ventricles in the brain, and in a healthy person the cerebrospinal fluid continuously circulates providing protection around the brain and spinal column, and is eventually absorbed into the bloodstream. There is no cure for hydrocephalus. Treatment is by way of inserting a fine tube known as a shunt, resembling a long thin strand of cooked tubular spaghetti.

Inserted through the skull into Chiara's fourth ventricle, the shunt was fed beneath the skin down the side of her neck and into the peritoneal cavity (a space within the abdomen) with a tiny 'chamber' and 'reservoir' attached to the shunt, positioned barely visible, behind her ear.

Although I hadn't been able to hold Chiara, we shared a special bond from the moment she was born. Regardless of the hour, I often experienced a compulsion to go to her. I sensed she needed reassurance. Able to detect depression at times, it was painfully obvious she longed to be held, yet seemingly she understood it wasn't possible.

Sometimes, on approaching her crib, she appeared sad and withdrawn, and as she detected my presence an air of contentment surrounded her. At times she even smiled. I don't care what anyone says, a baby can smile at any age. If they can yawn, sneeze and cry, they can certainly smile. There's a definite difference between the grimace of pain and happy contentment. Chiara also responded by opening her eyes and looking around whenever her big sister entered the room, before Dani even spoke or touched her.

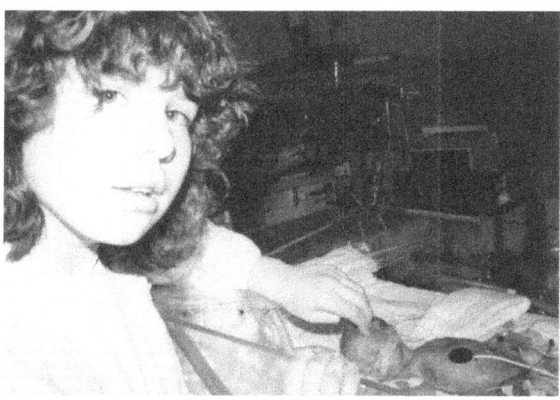

*Dani aged 14...with Chiara beneath the plastic film*

Appreciating the seriousness of the approaching surgery, staff aimed for us to have the joy of a cuddle. Our first attempt failed when Chiara stopped breathing. If it was detrimental to her health I didn't need a cuddle. It was more important that she preserve all her strength, and I didn't want our first cuddle to be one of trauma.

The team decided the time was right to try again. My instinct told me they wanted us to have a cuddle because they worried about her surviving the neurosurgery. It took four people, each playing a vital role to lift her out of the crib. As the plastic film was slowly peeled back I couldn't believe my ears.

Not only was she crying but for the first time I could hear her. I should have been upset but it was the most beautiful sound I had heard since Dani's first cry. Born before she was able to cry she sounded like a newborn kitten. Lifted out of the crib, with calculated timing she was tenderly placed in my arms. It was a strange moment. Although cradling her I couldn't feel her; she didn't weigh anything.

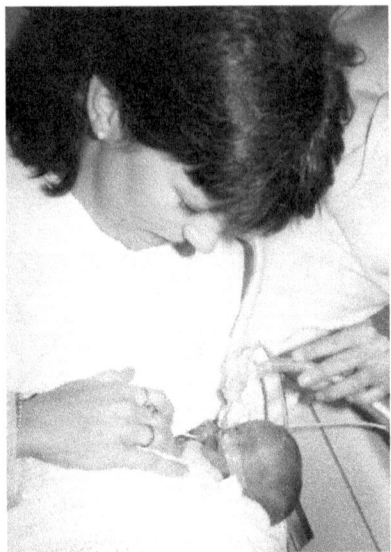

*First Cuddle 10 days old*

Too scared to breathe, I didn't dare move while I strained to look at her through my tears. It was probably only about thirty seconds but that time would be remembered and treasured forever. Back in her crib, I again thought of Gary. I didn't want anything more to do with him but it didn't give me the right to deprive Chiara of her father. I rang to invite him to meet her.

Knowing it may be my only chance to make it happen, I took a deep breath telling him how ill she was, that she required neurosurgery, and if he ever wished to meet his daughter he should do so that day. After initially stating he was too busy, then said he could only stay five minutes, agreed to meet me out the front of the hospital. I led him to Chiara's crib and stepped back. As doctors gathered discussing the surgery, Gary stood mesmerised. In silence he stared at his daughter for approximately two hours before ultimately saying he had to leave.

# *Neurosurgery nightmare begins*

Chiara would have to be transported across to the children's hospital so the question on everyone's lips was, would she survive the trip let alone neurosurgery. Watching her placed into what the hospital affectionately called Norris, which, from memory stands for Neo-Natal Retrieval and Resuscitation Intensive Care Service, was heart wrenching.

*NORRIS aka POPEYE*

The staff and I were filled with apprehension, wondering if we'd ever return, as the contraption containing Chiara was wheeled out of the room. My mother beside me, I tried to convince myself it resembled a submarine, and I nicknamed it Popeye but something was tearing at me. 'Popeye' resembled a coffin and to make it worse, as she was lifted into the back of the ambulance it was like a coffin being lifted into a hearse. Although treated and handled with the utmost dignity and respect I agonised over whether I'd see my baby alive again.

The emotion was intense as the accompanying doctor climbed on board with the nursing sister. He suggested I wait by the phone at home. As Chiara wasn't a patient at the children's hospital there was nowhere deemed suitable for me to wait, which I found astounding.

Not able to be there for her was sheer torture. I vowed Chiara would never again make a trip like that without me. The surgery was essential but the Queen Victoria Hospital didn't have the facilities for neurosurgeons. When Mr Hanieh informed me Chiara required neurosurgery my line of thinking changed. Instead of begging her to live, I questioned whether I wanted her to live for her benefit, or mine. I told her she didn't have to worry about me anymore. I couldn't bear to see her suffer and if she wanted to give up her fight I would somehow find the strength and courage to understand.

The call came to say she survived, was recovering well and on her way back to the Queen Victoria Hospital. The relief was immeasurable but the one time she needed me the most, I wasn't there.

On the twelfth day Dr O'Loughlin and I both agreed I was physically ready to leave the hospital. The time had come, and although there wasn't any reason for me to occupy a hospital bed any longer and although I looked forward to being with Dani, I dreaded leaving and having to go home to an empty nursery. Undergoing an emergency caesarean rendered me unable to drive for six weeks so my parents insisted it was best if Dani and I both stayed in their home until I regained my strength.

They would drive us back and forth to the hospital. Doing so allowed Dani to continue her schooling without too many interruptions. My father, with a pet hate of hospitals took over the school drop off and pick up. He would bring Dani into me when she had finished her homework each night.

Residing with my parents within five minutes of the hospital was a tremendous consolation and helped me immensely. Chiara was twelve days old and I was like a robot. Whatever was happening in the outside world was irrelevant even though in the past I had always watched the News on television and read the daily papers, I just didn't care anymore. Existing in this world I knew nothing about, my mental state was one of confusion and questioning.

Greg, my older brother, often drove the considerable distance from his home at night to collect me, and we visited Chiara together.

My older sister Teresa and my younger brother Trevor were both living in Melbourne. They kept in constant touch, visiting their tiniest niece as often as they could. We had our differences or more like all-out brawls as kids but as adults we share an unbreakable bond. The support of family and friends was exceptional, even though I felt alone I wasn't. No-one around me had experienced the torment of a very premature birth and consequently there still wasn't anyone I could seek advice from.

Within a few days of surgery, Chiara's head again developed an oval appearance. I stood silently as Mr Hanieh declared the shunt had blocked and she must immediately return to theatre. The neurosurgical procedure she was to undergo was known as a shunt revision.

The traumatic trip back to the children's hospital would be repeated but this time I went too. On arrival I realised what the nurse had meant when she said there wasn't anywhere for me to wait. Situated at the time, on the sixth floor, the corridors leading to the operating theatre were dark and I wondered why there weren't any lights on. It was a very depressing place to be. There wasn't so much as a chair anywhere but I didn't care. I was there, and I was as near to my baby as I could be.

While standing in the corridor Dr Sainsbury, an anaesthetist approached, and led me to his nearby office. He offered me his chair brought me a coffee, and told me he would return as soon as he had news that Chiara was in recovery. I was full of appreciation for his lovely gesture, and true to his word, he returned with the news I was hoping for.

Eventually a new bright and airy theatre was built on the third floor, and few years later I smiled to myself when I noticed a seat placed just outside the door. Things were slowly improving.

***

With nothing else to do my thoughts kept reflecting back to Gary and the many questions I had. I realised the only person who would know many of the answers other than him was his wife. There wasn't any point attempting to get the truth out of him, so when Chiara stabilised I mustered the strength and paid her a visit. Heavily pregnant with twins, she invited me inside. I didn't hold any malice towards her, as she too was caught in his web.

Both of us in tears, we calmly discussed our situation and I explained how her husband told me he was in the midst of getting a divorce. I told her I had no reason to doubt him and that we'd been in a relationship for eighteen months where I saw him almost daily. She asked if I wanted him back and I assured her she could keep him. By the time I left she had more answers than me and was shocked to learn that they were apparently in the middle of a divorce, and that he was determined to keep the house.

I felt empathy and compassion for her. I quietly hoped we could develop a friendship for the sake of the children considering they share the same father, and we would probably be seeing a bit of each other over the years to come, as they played together during access visits. However I would soon learn Gary and his wife didn't have any intention of his daughter ever meeting her siblings. They were depriving all the children of their basic right and I presume they stand proud of their decision. (Gary's wife gave birth to a third son before they divorced).

***

Days later, adversity struck when Mr Hanieh discovered a cyst developing at the base of Chiara's brain. It was impossible to remove so he inserted a tube into it and connected it to the existing shunt, thus enabling the ventricle and the cyst to drain into the peritoneal (abdominal) cavity. He referred to it as a 'piggyback' shunt.

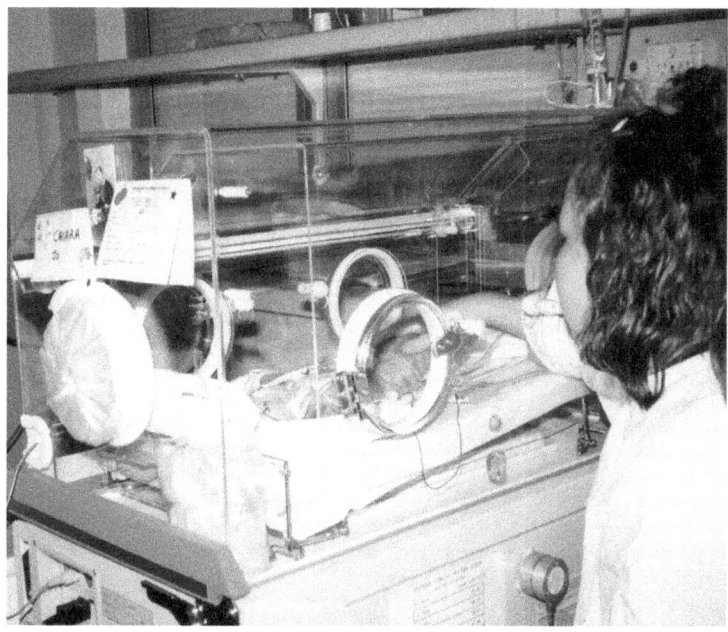

*Chiara is promoted to a Humidi-Crib with Dani at her side*

Chiara had stabilised and was promoted to a humidi-crib. It was a major step forward. Eventually she was moved to the back section of Intensive Care ready to take the next step through the door and into the Special Care Unit. Confident for the first time, Dr Viggy said he believed at six weeks of age Chiara could possibly survive. He went on to say he didn't know how she had made it that far, that it hadn't been through medical intervention and technology but more likely my continual presence at her side, and a miracle.

The decision was made to escort me on a tour through the remaining areas of the Nursery. At that time the Intensive Care Unit was referred to as 'level three' nursery, and the special care unit next door, referred to as 'level two.' The babies in there were noticeably bigger than those in 'level three' Intensive Care. Next we progressed through to the premature nursery, or 'level one,' designed to accommodate healthy premature babies prior to discharge.

Walking through the observation nursery where full term babies are checked and weighed, I was alarmed at their size wondering how any woman could give birth to such a huge baby. Seeing my horror the nurse asked what was wrong. I responded that I was shocked at the size of them. She laughed saying they were only seven and eight pound babies (approximately three kilograms). I had been around two pound babies (approximately one kilogram) for so long I forgot Dani was born the same size as the gigantic babies.

## *All babies are tiny*

As time progressed I became confident that while Chiara had a soft fontanel I would know when a shunt blocked. I discovered each time the fontanel began to fill and round off it would reduce down to normal within an hour of lifting her out of the crib. Something I was finally permitted to do. Doctors didn't give much credence to me at first, until I proved it to them. I showed them her fontanel while it was full and on taking her out for a cuddle asked them to return in an hour so they could witness the result themselves

For me it was common sense, the shunt acting as a drain would work better if she was nursed at an angle so I asked Mr Hanieh if he had any objections to me placing her on a bouncinette, realising it would have to be a doll's size as she was too small for a *real* one. Smiling he said, 'Helen if it works let's try it.' I was shocked he agreed as I expected him to say it was a silly idea.

Leaving the hospital I headed for the nearest toy shop and as I stood studying the toy bouncinettes the sales assistant approached.

'May I help you Madam?'

'Yes please, I need a doll's bouncinette but I'm not sure whether this one will be big enough.'

While visualising Chiara's size in comparison to the bouncinette, the assistant continued.

'Well how big is the doll?'

On answering that it was for my baby the look on his face was priceless.

'Madam you're in the wrong shop. You need a baby shop. These bouncinettes are for dolls not babies.'

Undaunted I tried to explain my baby was born three months prematurely and was very tiny.

'Oh Madam *all* babies are tiny.'

Shaking his head at me, I paid him ten dollars, and left him to his consternation. I was happy to have found a little pink doll's bouncinette.

Positioning Chiara on her new bouncinette, I was surprised to see she was too small for it. After a few slight adjustments she happily spent time on it until she grew into a *real* one, approximately three months later. She loved watching everyone around her and was soon waving her arms.

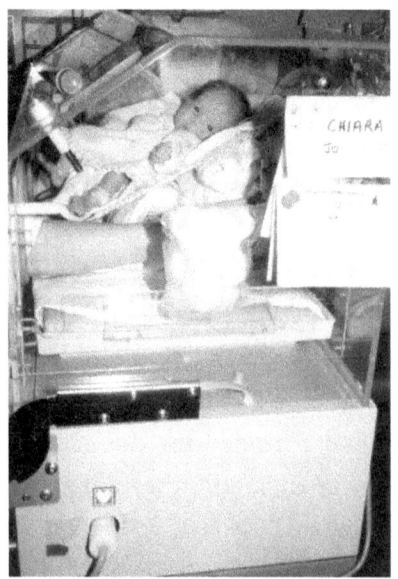

*Chiara on her Doll's Bouncinette inside the Humidi Crib wearing Doll's Clothes*

Seeing how content Chiara was in her bouncinette I began to feel sorry for the other babies who were tightly swaddled 24-hours-a-day. They were only turned from one side to the other having nothing to look at but the crib next to them.

***

While Chiara was on the bouncinette inside a humidi-crib sporting a bandage wrapped around her head, a member of staff from Channel Nine television station approached me seeking permission to film her as part of an advertisement promoting their fundraising Telethon Quest.

If appearing on television or in newspapers could help to raise money there was no way I would object. It would be the first of many appearances in the media, as a number of television and newspaper journalists began to follow Chiara's inspirational journey.

## Two hospitals unite

Before long I was disappointed to notice Chiara's fontanel had 'rounded off' again. The bouncinette didn't do anything to stop the shunt blocking but she was happy so we continued to nurse her on it. On raising my concern to the staff they agreed to monitor her closely. It wasn't long before they were contacting Mr Hanieh. The shunt had blocked and I noticed before the team did. I was beginning to recognise subtle changes in her demeanour.

Mr Hanieh immediately organised shunt function studies to be carried out in the Nuclear Medicine Department of the children's hospital while Queen Victoria Hospital staff once again deployed 'Popeye' to transport her across town. When we arrived, the nurses searched for a heater as the room in nuclear medicine was cold. While waiting for a nurse to return with a heater, Chiara was wrapped in aluminium foil to stop her body temperature dropping dangerously low. I had only ever used aluminium foil and plastic film to wrap food in, and there I stood watching my baby wrapped up like a food parcel to help save her life.

While Chiara was laying in 'Popeye,' an insensitive female nurse, displaying an unpleasant attitude, approached. Glaring in at Chiara, she squealed, 'Oh my God! Hey, everyone come and look at this.'

Appalled at her insensitivity, I moved to where she was standing to put some space between her and Chiara.

Outraged I questioned her in disgust. 'Do you mind?'

'What's the matter?' she asked.

Scowling, my eyes fixed on hers with a stare resolving to pierce her soul; she was left in no doubt.

'Oh, are *you* its mother?'

'As a matter of fact I am, and my baby isn't an 'it' on display for your benefit.'

Backing away, she quickly disappeared.

\*\*\*

The function study was carried out by firstly shaving some of Chiara's hair then, using a syringe, a small amount of cerebral spinal fluid was taken from the shunt chamber behind her ear for testing.

Radioactive dye was then injected directly into her shunt. The specialists were watching closely on a monitor as it drained through the shunt system revealing the blockage. Chiara was rushed back into theatre. Sometimes after a function study, she returned to the ward a great deal happier than before. It led me to wonder, in ignorance, whether the radioactive dye could actually be helping a small blockage to clear.

There were times the function studies returned a negative result. They were not always capable of revealing a shunt malfunction. Luckily for his patients, the brilliant Mr Hanieh didn't place his entire trust in technology and equipment and sometimes operated based solely on his own unquestionable expertise.

Neurosurgery completed, Chiara was admitted into Rose Ward at the children's hospital where babies are cared for, to recuperate before being transported back to the Queen Victoria Hospital. The monitors started beeping, and being straight out of surgery it was to be expected. The nurse in attendance stabilised her but within minutes the monitors reactivated. Seconds later they were going crazy. I had known them to go off within an hour or so but not so often in a matter of seconds.

The doctor in charge of Chiara's care at the children's hospital had been watching closely from the desk and came to see what was happening. In a whisper he asked, 'What's wrong Sister?'

'I'm not sure but I don't like it.'

'No, I don't either,' he said. The room was filling with people, something wasn't right, and while I didn't know what all the other doctors were doing, they did. 'Helen it's best if you leave the room I'll come and get you once I've fixed the problem.'

'Doctor what is it, what's wrong?' I asked.

'It seems your baby has been given too much morphine. I must reverse it immediately please wait outside, I'll come and get you.'

'No doctor please let me stay I won't be in the way I promise. You do whatever you have to, *please* don't make me leave, she needs me. Please don't send me out, *please*.' I begged.

Continuing to work as we spoke he agreed, allowing me to stay. Tears flowing I pleaded with God not to take her as the team worked against the morphine. Her doctor let out a huge sigh of relief turned to me and smiled.

'Helen I think she'll be alright now.'

'Thank you so much. I can't believe it, as if she hasn't had enough to contend with. How did this even happen? If I'm going to lose her, I'd never accept an overdose! How can I ever thank you for saving her life?'

The next day Chiara returned to the Queen Victoria Hospital. I was feeling slightly more confident as she steadily progressed. The time had come for Dani and I to move out of my parents' home and return to our own. It meant travelling an extra fifteen minutes. We continued to eat our meals at their house and they did our washing and ironing, which helped to keep the pressure off me having to run a household. I didn't feel ready, physically or psychologically to do that but wanted to be in my own home to enable us to return to some form of normality.

No sooner had Dani and I arrived home for our first night in many weeks, the phone rang. It was Dr Sam, one of her doctors compelled to call with bad news. Sometimes I wondered if Dr Sam ever slept. He was amazing and always seemed to be there. While carrying out routine checks he noticed clear fluid leaking through the suture line from Chiara's previous shunt revision. He was only ringing to inform me it had happened, and with Mr Hanieh consulted, insisted she wasn't in immediate danger.

Regardless of his reassurance I had to return to the hospital to be with her. A pressure bandage which had been placed around her head resembled a turban. She was being closely monitored. I considered it wasn't anything too drastic to worry about and was much more at ease being with her. It enabled me to see for myself that she was fine.

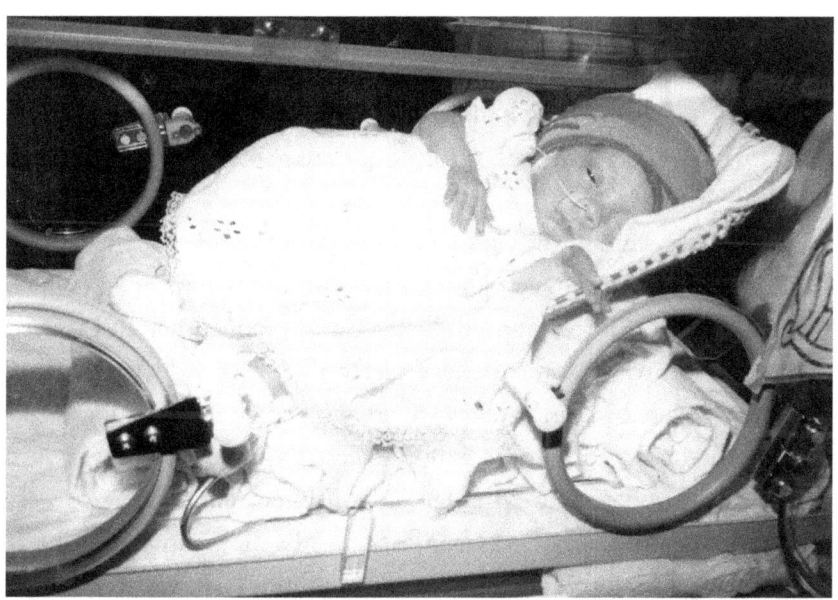

*Wearing her turban putting her hand out to be held*

\*\*\*

At six weeks Chiara was transferred into the Special Care Unit. It was a momentous occasion, another milestone not only for her but the entire team. Everyone was visibly moved as they congratulated and farewelled us on our shift into the adjoining unit. It took time getting used to the new section as Chiara shared a nurse with one, and sometimes two, other babies. The one-to-one ratio was only allocated to Intensive Care babies.

It soon became a case of revolving doors as each time Chiara deteriorated she was re-admitted into Intensive Care, until she was considered well enough to progress through to the premature nursery. I didn't feel comfortable being there. I had been used to Chiara receiving so much attention in Intensive Care, that there seemed to be scant support in the premature nursery. That wasn't the case though; it was just a matter of me becoming acquainted with a new way of life, with Chiara deemed well enough to no longer require intensive or special care.

However, she had only been in the premature unit for less than a week, when one morning Dani, my mother and I were strolling towards her. I stopped dumbfounded. Dani moved around me to see why I had come to a standstill. On the verge of tears, I blurted, 'Oh no Mum, Chiara's not right.' Squeezing my hand my mother stood silently.

The nurses were in the middle of handover. 'Carol, Chiara is grey!' I called out. Offering no apology for the outburst I continued, 'Quick help her please.' Chaos erupted. Sister Carol grabbed her and started giving suction while someone else raced off to get a doctor. Within seconds we were back in Intensive Care with suspected meningitis.

One of the doctors immediately injected antibiotics straight into the shunt chamber, with Mr Hanieh consulted. Emergency surgery arranged, the meningitis was confined inside the shunt and Chiara was once again admitted back into the children's hospital to undergo another round of neurosurgery, recover and stabilise, before returning to the Queen Victoria Hospital, again.

The following day I arrived early in time to give Chiara her morning feed. I asked the nurse if I could have a comfortable chair and a pillow as I have arthritis in my spine. The nurse disappeared; I thought she went to find me a chair. Sometime later a woman appeared who I didn't know. She was telling me it wasn't possible to breastfeed. I asked why. 'You can't do that here.'

'But *why?*' I asked.

'Because you *can't.*'

'But *why* can't I feed my baby?' I was fighting back tears.

'Because we *can't* allow you to do that.'

'But the Queen Vic doctors said it's important and I want to. I've been feeding her for a couple of weeks, so please just explain what problem will I cause?'

'I've *already* told you, you can't do it.'

By this time I was becoming agitated. 'Well *who* are *you?* I'd like to speak to my daughter's doctor as I'm sure there's been a misunderstanding. It would be in the notes and I'm positive it'll be alright to continue. Please go and check, this is important for both of us.'

The woman scowled saying 'I *am* her doctor.' She then left.

We were in a side room and there weren't any other patients with us. It wasn't as though I would be offending anyone. Bewildered I was forced to accept her condemnation.

Later in the day over the public address system I heard Dr Lamb being paged. He was another of Chiara's dedicated and respected doctors from the Queen Victoria Hospital visiting the children's hospital. Ironically it was Dr Lamb who requested a breastfeeding program be set up for me at the Queen Victoria Hospital. I was sure he could help me sort the problem out. I ran to the public phone and immediately contacted him. He was flabbergasted that I wasn't permitted to feed Chiara and soon rectified the situation. I thanked him profusely and returned to feed Chiara.

The following day we were back at the Queen Victoria Hospital but not trusted to stay healthy, Chiara wouldn't progress past the Special Care Unit. Within days she was back in 'Popeye' and transported back to theatre at the children's hospital with yet another blocked shunt, and then re-admitted into a ward there.

While sitting next to her the monitors sounded the all too familiar beeping noise. I watched calmly, knowing what to expect. The nurse assigned to her would gently pat her, while at the same time, pause the monitors and Chiara would rally. When the nurse became flustered and red faced, eyes welling and clearly panicking, I asked what was wrong.

Chiara appeared to be having another bradycardia whereby her heart rate dropped setting off the alarms. Without a word, the nurse continued fumbling with the oxygen unable to get it to work properly.

'I can't get it. I can't get it,' she repeated.

Not prepared to wait any longer I began patting Chiara while calmly asking, 'Nurse what are you trying to do?'

Looking at me, the nurse could see I had settled Chiara. She had a look of disbelief or relief on her face, I'm not sure which.

'Chiara was having a braddy, aren't you familiar with them?'

She didn't answer me.

'Nurse, she does this all the time. All you have to do is pat her and if that doesn't work, gently knock on the side of the cot. She's doesn't usually need the oxygen.'

The Clinical Nurse Consultant (CNC) came in to see what all the fuss was about.

Conscious of not wanting to sound smug, I said 'Chiara was only having a braddy and nurse had trouble getting the oxygen to work. I told her to just pat her, or if that fails to knock on the cot until she rallies.'

'That's right. Is Chiara ok now?' she asked.

'Yes, she is thank you.'

Although I felt sorry for the nurse, and at the risk of sounding like a know-all who knows nothing, I was disappointed she didn't know what to do.

***

On the third day I wondered why we were still there and hadn't been transferred back to the Queen Victoria Hospital. I queried the nurse. 'I don't know but I'll find out for you,' she said.

A doctor appeared in the doorway. 'Your daughter isn't going back to the Queen Vic.'

'Pardon?'

'Your daughter isn't going back to the Queen Vic. They don't want her back.'

'What? This has to be a mistake, what do you mean they don't want her back; they would never say that. If she weren't going to return Dr Viggy would've told me himself. I was only talking to him this morning and her cot is still there. *Who* said they don't want her back?'

'She's not their problem anymore.'

'What do you mean problem?'

'She's not their problem anymore, she's our problem now.'

I was gobsmacked at the aloofness. 'But I don't understand.'

'She's too big for the Queen Vic now and with neurosurgical issues she belongs here so she won't be going back.'

'But does Dr Viggy know?'

'I presume he does, I spoke to one of the doctors at the Queen Vic this morning and it was decided Chiara would be better left here.'

'Well *who* did you speak to because her doctors wouldn't do this without telling me?'

'It doesn't matter *who* decided it, the fact is *she's staying.*'

'I don't believe it. I'm going to see Dr Viggy.'

Feeling as though we had been thrown out of the Queen Victoria Hospital, I can't begin to describe the raging emotion. I 'flew' down to my car. Distressed I arrived at the door of the Intensive Care Unit at the Queen Victoria Hospital and rang the bell.

'Hi Helen when are you and Chiara coming back? We thought you'd be back here by now.'

'It seems we're not coming back. Please, where's Dr Viggy?'

'Helen what on earth has happened? Whatever is wrong, you look terrible. How's Chiara?'

'Oh she's fine thank you but where's Dr Viggy?'

'He's gone home, he had a rough night, can I help?'

I then noticed one of Chiara's long term room-mates wasn't in his crib. 'Where's baby xxx?'

'Dr Viggy and the team were here all night and did all they could. Dr Viggy is devastated he's gone home to rest but he'll be back later.'

Finding out that a precious tiny baby had just died, my problem was insignificant. A young single mum, just like me was suffering the tragic loss of her little boy and my heart went out to her. Everyone was upset and there I stood worrying about what hospital Chiara should be in.

'Oh God I had no idea.'

'Tell me, what's wrong Helen, perhaps I can help?' My distress was somewhat pathetic in comparison to the events preceding my visit. Feeling despondent I mumbled, 'The doctor at the children's is adamant you don't want Chiara back here anymore.'

'Helen what are you talking about? Look there, her crib and belongings are where you left them, of course she's coming back. Dr Viggy isn't here but I'll call Dr McPhee he'll sort it out.'

'Who's Dr McPhee?'

'Oh he's really lovely you'll like him. I'm surprised you haven't met him yet. Wait here and don't worry Chiara *is* coming back. We're expecting her.'

'Helen, this is Dr Andy McPhee.'

'Oh doctor, I am so sorry I know I've come at a terrible time. You probably can't help me I don't even know you and you don't know Chiara.'

'Oh yes, I certainly *do* know Chiara. I've looked after your daughter quite a few times. She's an amazing little girl. What can I do to help you?'

'A doctor at the Children's told me the Queen Vic don't want her back. Is it true?'

'Helen, there has apparently been a misunderstanding. Of course she's coming back. Her crib is ready and waiting. Normally by her age she would stay at the children's but sometimes there has to be an exception. She's *our* baby and will be discharged home from here when we're happy with her progress. If you prefer to stay at the children's it can be arranged but you obviously want her to come back here. I'll ring Dr Matthews and have her transferred today.'

'Oh thank you. You can't imagine what it was like hearing you didn't want her back. I didn't know what to think. I'm so relieved, thank you so much.'

That day formed the basis of a wonderful on-going friendship between Dr Andy, Chiara and I, as we happily settled back in amongst friends.

***

Shyness making way for assertiveness, I could feel myself changing and becoming stronger as Chiara's life depended on me stepping up to become her advocate but it was emotionally and physically exhausting. It was then I realised the two hospitals must unite. It was 1987 and we were fast approaching the nineties. Not only were tiny babies subjected to travelling to and fro but it was imperative the Queen Victoria Hospital Neo-Natal trained staff, continued the care of their infants regardless of which hospital they were at.

Unbeknown to me at that time, talks were already under way to amalgamate both hospitals. A public meeting was called and I felt obliged to attend so I invited the mother who had been brought in from Modbury Hospital and shared my room in the High Dependency ward, to accompany me. While our tiny babies were fighting for life, people were fighting to save the Queen Victoria Hospital and I became angry at what I was hearing.

I sat, I listened and I was torn. That hospital had been my world but it wasn't the building helping to save my baby, it was the outstanding devotion of the staff and life-saving equipment within that building. The problem was it didn't have the facilities necessary to prevent critically ill babies from being put through the trauma of being transported across the other side of town to the children's hospital for surgery.

As people in the room were engaging in heated argument with many angered about the possibility of an amalgamation, I had enough. Frustrated and fuming I stood up and asked, 'What are you people wanting to save here, a building or children's lives?'

The room fell silent. I couldn't believe I did that. Then I was asked to share my story and reason for attending the meeting.

With raw emotion and tears falling I explained what we were going through and how distressing and traumatic it was, continuously being transported across to the children's hospital and the anxiety, problems and stress it created. I was astounded at the applause. At the end of the meeting I was shocked when approached and invited to become a member of the Consumer Consultant Steering Committee to help oversee the amalgamation process.

Following that initial meeting I received several invitations to join committees, which I did over the years. I think they regretted having me on a particular committee one day, when the members were excited about wanting to put a large bronze logo worth many thousands of dollars on the play deck of the children's hospital.

I was infuriated that anyone would happily waste thousands of dollars on a useless logo while children were forced to share vital medical equipment and basic items on the wards. I asked the committee members if they really thought parents would be as thrilled as they were to see a huge chunk of very expensive bronze on the play deck, while their seriously ill children waited in turn to share monitors etc. The order wasn't placed.

# *Home at last*

To help myself feel normal again before Chiara came home, I needed something to do in the evenings to stop myself reflecting on what we'd been through. I wanted to look forward to a future enjoying both my daughters. I settled on investing in some cheap wallpaper, and set about transforming our otherwise dull, colourless and boring abode.

Every night, regardless of the hour I arrived home, I hung at least one roll of wallpaper. Concentrating on the job helped me partially switch off and by the time Chiara came home I had a house full of papered walls.

Our lengthy stay in the Queen Victoria Hospital was a combination of mixed emotions and some degree of depression watching other babies thrive and leave with their families, often before their expected departure date. Although happy for them, deep down I was jealous, wishing each time it was us. I wondered whether our turn would ever come.

While holding Chiara, a nursing sister, who I hadn't previously met, casually stated she would be discharging her the following week. I presumed she had made a mistake. Prior to that moment, going home hadn't ever been mentioned and there stood a nurse in front of me, confused at my reaction.

Our dreams were beginning to materialise. Chiara *is* going to be discharged home but will we make it out the door or will she get sick again? I couldn't get excited, anything could go wrong but I strived to be positive. A room had been booked for us in Lee Wing, an area designated to accommodate mothers and their babies, prior to discharge, who had spent all their time in one of the nurseries without an opportunity to spend a night together alone. If any problems were experienced there would be immediate backup from nursery staff.

One hundred days after Chiara's birth we celebrated with a surprise birthday cake supplied by the hospital, before taking up residence in Lee Wing. Sound asleep by 7pm it would be the first and last time Chiara slept all night until she reached the age of three. I sat watching her wishing she would make a sound. Her colour looked good and she was breathing, so I presumed she must have been alright or she wouldn't be so peaceful. I was tempted to wake her just to hold her. She was finally all mine, she was real, and we were going home. Filled with emotion I was reluctant to get excited as we weren't out the door yet.

At 8am on day 101 she finally awoke and I couldn't wait to feed, bathe and dress her in the pretty pink dress and booties I had bought for the special day that I never thought would come. Dani and my mother arrived at 9am to take us home. Although ecstatic, I was nervous as I packed up and headed back to the nursery to say our goodbyes. It was a poignant moment for each and every person who had played a vital role in saving Chiara's fragile life.

Thanking them all I then walked across to Dr Viggy. Hands outstretched he was adamant I shouldn't thank him, insisting once again, he believed Chiara only survived due to a miracle and my constant vigil. He reiterated it was the bond we formed that brought her through the darkest days and not so much what he or medical technology had achieved.

Regardless of what he said, he was the best Paediatrician in the world to me and a significant and esteemed member of the extraordinary team of angels who saved my baby. Without him, Mr Hanieh and the dedicated Queen Victoria and children's hospital staff, I wouldn't have taken Chiara home, that is fact. Everyone was amazed, not only that we were leaving but that Chiara was healthy. We had all expected the worst but no one ever gave up hope.

An appointment had been made to have an assessment the following week by the Long Term Follow Up team. It meant we weren't thrown out into the world alone; we would continue to have the backup of the team for as long necessary. The fact the program was run by the same doctors and staff who cared for Chiara throughout her stay, gave me a tremendous sense of security because I didn't know what to expect from her after everything she went through.

I had been terrified at the thought that once we left the hospital we would be completely on our own. It was a huge relief having a nurse visit us at home on a weekly basis, and I always looked forward to hearing the encouraging words that Chiara was progressing better than expected. Between the visits, whenever I was concerned about any health issues, the medical and nursing staff were available and always happy to see us. I was never made to feel like I was a nuisance. The home visits became less frequent as the months passed but Chiara's development continued to be monitored by the Long Term Follow Up team until she reached the age of ten.

\*\*\*

Since birth Chiara had suffered with reflux and doctors tried a variety of treatments to no avail. I asked what they wanted to achieve by putting different medications into her bottles. The response was to thicken the feeds to help ease the reflux. Concluding we had nothing to lose, I began adding Farex baby cereal to her bottles instead of the cocktail of medications, and we never looked back.

# PART TWO

# *A mother's intuition*

At home the nursery came alive with the sound of gurgles, noisy toys, the scent of baby lotions and piles of nappies. We were finally able to settle into a lifestyle generally taken for granted with the arrival of a newborn. Snuggled in Dani's hand-me-down well-travelled bassinette, Chiara slept next to my bed until she reached six months of age. Determined not to become paranoid, I then reluctantly put her in her own room to sleep.

One of the first things I did when settled back at home was to organise a traditional baptism. Father Farmer agreed to conduct the service and it was attended by our entire family in Saint Ignatius Church at Norwood.

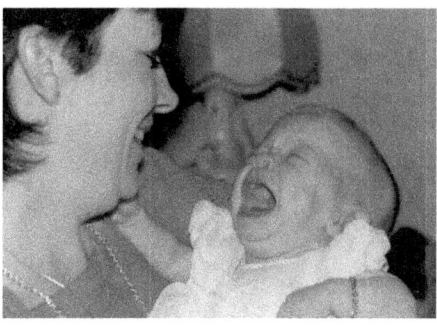

*Chiara's Baptism Day*

Early one morning, after we'd been at home for a couple of months, Chiara woke up vomiting. I knew instinctively the shunt had blocked. Without hesitation, I picked her up, woke Dani and we raced off to the children's hospital where staff asked what was wrong. I was terrified as it was the first time her shunt had blocked since we left the security of the Neo-Natal team. I was lost and vulnerable, scared in unfamiliar surroundings.

Prior to our departure from the Queen Victoria Hospital the last thing I asked was what I should say if we ever had to present to the children's hospital with a blocked shunt. Following the instructions given, I explained Chiara was well known to Mr Hanieh, had been born three months premature, undergone a number of shunt revisions, and I believed the ventricular peritoneal shunt had blocked. I wasn't prepared for the response, 'How would *you* know you're only the mother!'

Presenting with vomiting, irritability and sleepiness, she was diagnosed with a probable case of gastroenteritis. My intuition was screaming shunt but how could I question medical and nursing professionals when I was *only* a mother?

Disillusioned, we left the Casualty Department with her still very ill. Frightened and frustrated I sat in the car, eager to consult with Mr Hanieh but not knowing how to get in touch with him, we returned home.

Two hours later we reappeared in the Casualty Department, and although nervous, I maintained I wasn't leaving until I spoke to Mr Hanieh. I had to find the courage to be assertive and challenge nursing staff and interns or risk the consequences. Without further resistance the phone call was made and Mr Hanieh in turn asked to speak to me which resulted in an urgent scan revealing that which I already knew.

# *Expect the unexpected*

At the age of nine months (corrected back to six, due to the three-month prematurity), Chiara sat unaided. By eleven months she was crawling; talking at twelve months, and walking at sixteen months. By eighteen months, much to our surprise, she was putting lengthy sentences together. Strangers stopped us in the street to comment on her speech; they couldn't believe someone so tiny could talk.

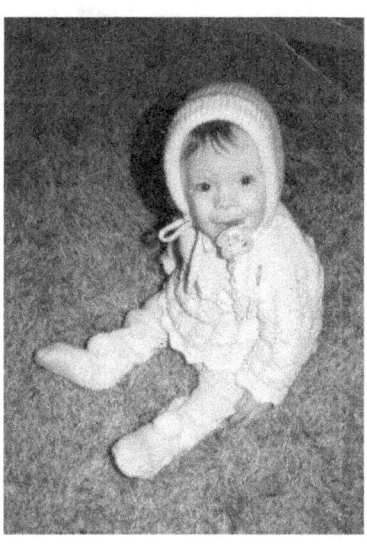

*Chiara nine months old*

In between shunt revisions we made the most of each day, delighting in being home, cherishing our fun times, appreciating hospital-free days. Shopping soon became a challenge though. The child everyone dreads in a supermarket was my Chiara refusing to take 'no' for an answer, while throwing her own items in the trolley. Her determination was shining through everyday life. How could I complain when it was her sheer determination that saved her life so many times.

Shopping excursions were often cut short if Chiara started vomiting, and I knew the other two symptoms would quickly follow. It meant leaving a trolley load of groceries where they were, to race off to hospital. I have often wondered what supermarket staff thought when they came across a fully laden trolley left abandoned in their aisles.

Vomiting is an unmistakable symptom of a shunt blockage, accompanied with irritability and sleepiness. On presentation of all three symptoms in succession, it becomes obvious to me the shunt is causing problems. My intuition plays a definite part, enabling me to differentiate between a basic illness, and shunt malfunction.

When Chiara was eleven months old I was mortified when it was suggested she would qualify for the Disability Allowance. My baby having a disability hadn't entered my head. I thought all she had to do was to stay well. I hadn't considered the aftermath of her traumatic birth, would result in her having any on-going or permanent disabilities, so I was stunned at the suggestion. Reassured the allowance was a means to help ease the financial burden I reluctantly applied and it was granted. However, I didn't expect to go through the stress of proving to the Government every year for many years thereafter, that she required a great deal more care and attention than any other child her age.

For her first birthday we celebrated with a party, inviting everyone who had played a major role in our lives and her progress. Chiara survived that first year thanks to many people and quietly spent her special day taking it all in her stride, not knowing what to make of so many people congregating in her home.

Enjoying the attention, she went about opening her presents, keeping a watchful eye on all the other children who were taking over her room, toys and cubby house. Coaxing her to remove the dummy to blow out one large candle was deemed an impossible mission. Chiara didn't have any intention of giving up 'nummy' for anyone or anything. She had developed a strong personality and was articulate, methodical and very loving, possessing a happy disposition but so very determined to always have her own way.

Soon after her birthday, as I sat watching television one evening, there was a knock on the door. I was completely taken aback to see Gary standing on the front porch. As I let him in he was apologising for all the pain and hurt he caused declaring he had left his wife - again - and sought to make amends for what he put us through. With my head swirling I didn't know what to think or what to say or do, and just sat listening to him. Minutes later someone was blasting their car horn in the driveway. I went out to investigate but couldn't see who it was, so I called out, 'Who is it?'

'Is Gary there?' An angry female voice bellowed.

'Hang on I'll get him for you.'

Life had become even more complicated and I only wished to be left in peace.

After his wife left I asked, 'I thought you said you'd left her. What do you want from me? Why are you doing this to us, don't you know how cruel it is to play with someone's emotions?'

'Helen listen to me, it's over. You, Chiara and Dani are who I want to be with.'

'But you have twins now, how could you leave them?'

'It's okay, I'll still see them, look I have a photo.'

His two boys and Chiara could have been triplets; the resemblance uncanny even though they were boys and Chiara a girl with different mothers. My head was telling me to throw him out but my heart ached for my youngest daughter; he was her daddy but his unexpected reappearance sickened me.

Dani had grown up with an absent father and I wasn't going to stand between Chiara and her father if he wanted to play the doting dad. Over the following two weeks he was in our lives and I was in turmoil. It didn't feel right having him there but I was struggling with the guilt of depriving my baby girl of her father.

A few days after he had moved in, he left to visit his parents, or so he said, to apparently tell them of his plan to live with us. He was gone so long I started to think he wasn't coming back, when eventually he returned.

'I'm just getting my things,' he said and left but I didn't care. Chiara was asking for 'daddy' so I phoned him the next day to ask if he would maintain contact with her. He stated his wife agreed to have him back providing he never saw us again.

***

In February 1989 I became ill and in excruciating pain. A visit to Dr O'Loughlin resulted in my being admitted into the Queen Victoria Hospital as a matter of urgency where surgery took place that evening. He suspected an ovarian cyst required draining.

Hours later I awoke to his voice, 'Helen I'm so sorry it was much more serious than we thought.' Turning my head I could barely see him through the fog of the anaesthetic. The profound tone in his voice left me without doubt something had gone very wrong.

A mass of tumours, cysts and endometriosis, completely blocked tubes and my remaining ovary were removed. Everything except the uterus was eliminated, the operation marking the beginning of a long-term battle with Hormone Replacement Therapy. Experimenting with tablets, patches, monthly injections and implants to find the right treatment, I felt I was losing my mind doing and saying stupid things, and at times suffering panic attacks. I envied women who claimed hormone replacement was a wonder drug and could only imagine how bad their lives must have been before their hysterectomies.

While I was under anaesthetic it became undeniably certain I was facing a grim situation. Dr O'Loughlin was confronted with making critical decisions on my behalf. Possible to save the uterus, he asked each of the female nurses assisting him what they would want him to do if it were them in the same predicament. Four of the five advised removing everything which would naturally mark the end of my menstrual cycle. The fifth nurse stated if he was able to save it he should leave the uterus in place as, 'She'll miss not having her periods.'

Hearing that a few days later made me wonder how many women miss that part of their lives as I certainly wouldn't have. The deciding factor was the nagging thought perhaps one day I may want to try to conceive more children, therefore leaving the uterus would give me the option to utilise the IVF (In Vitro Fertilisation) program. Dr O'Loughlin believed I should be permitted the choice and considered the possibility I too may be of the same mind-set as the fifth nurse.

Accepting the gravity of the surgery helped me overcome any chance of feeling sorry for myself. I was lucky to be alive. Some nurses envied me, so I wasn't the only ignorant one in that hospital. I and it seems others, believed without tubes and ovaries it would be impossible to menstruate. I eventually asked Dr O'Loughlin what it meant to be left with only the uterus.

He explained my menstrual cycle would continue and although disappointed, I was pleased I asked or I would have thought I was haemorrhaging and panicked. Dr O'Loughlin informed me I must have been in that state for a minimum of five years, and that Chiara at only two years of age, had apparently been conceived through blocked tubes, endometriosis, tumours and a mangled mess. He re-affirmed his declaration that she was 'certainly a little miracle girl and meant to be here.'

Six months later I returned to hospital suffering tremendous pain insisting my uterus be removed. The following morning Dr O'Loughlin entered the room shaking his head.

'Helen, we would've thought it impossible without your ovaries but your uterus contained endometriosis, even though it was free of the disease when we operated only a few months ago. I should have known with you to expect the unexpected.'

Dani and Chiara were in the care of my parents and were brought in to visit most nights. When they arrived on the fifth night I immediately noticed Chiara wasn't right. I summoned the nurse to call Dr Viggy but he wasn't available so Dr Haslam responded. It didn't take him long to determine she was in serious trouble and would have to see Mr Hanieh but there wasn't any way I was going to let her go without me, nor put the responsibility on my parents.

It took some convincing that I was well enough, before Dr Haslam agreed to let me leave my hospital bed. I assured him I would take full responsibility for my own health. He contacted the children's hospital to alert them of our pending arrival and told staff they had to look after me as well. Weak from the surgery, I left with my family and moved into a side room in the children's hospital where two beds were waiting for us. Chiara with a blocked shunt diagnosis was rushed off for surgery. A few days later we both returned home to recuperate together.

Sensibility prevailed on the 15th March 1989 when the Queen Victoria Hospital physically amalgamated with the Adelaide Children's Hospital to become the Adelaide Medical Centre for Women and Children. It wasn't long before the name was shortened to the Women's and Children's Hospital, as it is known today, and the Casualty Department was renamed Emergency Department. (The Queen Victoria Hospital site was closed in 1995 and is now an apartment block).

The amalgamation solved the issue of transporting seriously ill babies but I continue to feel for families involved in car accidents, or situations that often leaves parents in one hospital, and children in another. I can imagine the distress it causes and look forward to witnessing the ultimate amalgamation of the Royal Adelaide Hospital and Women's and Children's Hospital which will herald the end of families being separated at the worst possible time in their lives.

(Almost thirty years later a new Royal Adelaide Hospital was opened in 2017. In 2018 the incoming State Liberal Party committed to build a new Women's and Children's Hospital on the same site by 2024, as against the outgoing Labor Party only promising a new women's hospital which in my opinion would have put us back 30 years, again having to transport seriously ill babies between hospitals. I told my story and made my opinion known to politicians on both sides as soon as I heard that plan, and basically begged them not to ever separate the hospitals again). I am however aware that at least a couple of South Australian doctors believe the amalgamation was a 'mistake' and only want the women's hospital rebuilt on the new Royal Adelaide Hospital site)

# *A father's denial*

Celebrating her second birthday, 11 July 1989, a family party at home had Chiara thoroughly enjoying herself as we relished in a relaxed, normal day. I began encouraging her to throw away the 'nummy' now that she was a big girl but she retaliated by sucking two at a time while managing to drink her bottle squeezed in between them.

*2nd Birthday 1989 within hours Chiara was undergoing neurosurgery*

By 10pm everyone had left and after putting a happy but tired Chiara to bed, Dani and I went into the lounge room. We were still up watching a movie at 1 o'clock in the morning when I thought I heard a familiar sound. I ran into Chiara's bedroom and was saddened to find her vomiting. Knowing instinctively it had nothing to do with anything she had eaten, Dani secured the house while I put Chiara in the car and we made a dash to hospital.

After spending three distressing hours in the Emergency Department convincing staff it was a shunt blockage, she was eventually admitted into Fielders Ward which specialised in neurosurgical patients, and again in the middle of the night Mr Hanieh was called upon. The shunt revised we returned home a few days later and life resumed its normal time bomb pattern with a few laughs and happy days in between.

Chiara loved to assist with housework and as fast as I could tidy up she followed behind pulling things out informing me she was helping too. I would allow her to wash the dishes and soon regret it. The minute my back was turned soapsuds would overflow as an empty bottle of detergent was held in her hand. Bath time was always a laugh with more bubbles and empty bottles. Housework when she was younger was undertaken at night with her tucked up in bed, except when she pretended to be asleep only to sneak out to get into more mischief.

Soon after her second birthday a car I recognised as Gary's pulled up and parked out the front of our house. Not again. What did he want *now*? What was he doing here?

'Helen I was hoping I could see Chiara.'

'She's asleep, anyway hasn't your wife forbidden you to see us?'

'Don't worry about that I'd really like to see her.' Lifting a sleepy girl out of her cot I whispered, 'daddy is here to see you.'

Sucking on two dummies and clutching her bottle it broke my heart as she sleepily whispered 'daddy' stretching her arms out to him. Gary stayed approximately two hours then left. He returned a week later, catching me home collecting some clothes, as Chiara was back in Intensive Care. He asked to follow me in his car so he could visit her.

After sitting at her cot for an hour he decided to go outside to have a cigarette and I went with him. While we were seated at a table on the play deck discussing her health issues two people approached.

'Hello Gary what are you doing here?'

'Oh I'm just here with a friend visiting her daughter.'

I was sickened to the core hearing him refer to Chiara as his friend's daughter, while she lay fighting for her life. It enraged me and I didn't know how to respond. I realised none of his friends would have been aware he had a little daughter. Excusing myself I returned to Chiara and he left.

As soon as were we home from the hospital he was back again. I hid my contempt and put up with his visits for Chiara's sake, until they became too frequent. He was spending less time with Chiara and more time talking to me in the hope of reviving our relationship.

He was visiting more than once a week and it was all getting too much for me. One day I asked whether he was there for his daughter or to see me, and if that were the case, not to bother coming back.

## *Intermittent shunt blockages*

As Chiara grew she underwent CAT scans (Computerised Axial Tomography) rather than shunt function studies to determine a malfunction and being so young, she required an anaesthetic to ensure she remained completely still. To help overcome her fear of the scanner, I nicknamed it the spaceship, and at the age of two I was confident she could understand that if she didn't move she wouldn't need an anaesthetic, which was the thing she hated most about the process.

Not sharing my confidence, Mr Hanieh reluctantly agreed to let us try. Chiara would do anything to avoid an anaesthetic and understood the consequences if she moved, so she vowed to stay absolutely still. Making good on her promise, she underwent her scan without an anaesthetic. Gas mask in hand the anaesthetist stood at the ready. Everyone was delighted Chiara didn't move for the entire duration of the scan.

Christmas Eve 1989 we were back in Fielders Ward and with Mr Hanieh away on holiday enjoying a well-earned break, Professor Simpson was covering for him. Although a scan revealed a blockage at the top end of the shunt he surprised me when he said surgery could wait. I remembered asking Mr Hanieh when Chiara first started neurosurgery, how much time I had to get her to hospital when she had a blockage and he told me it was best to have her there within two hours. I was confused by Professor Simpson's decision not to operate.

At 5pm we returned home to enjoy Christmas with instructions to return on the 26th December, to undergo a shunt revision. Professor Simpson insisted that I not hesitate to interrupt his Christmas dinner if Chiara deteriorated.

As we left the hospital, Father Christmas, resplendent in his red suit, complete with an enormous sack of toys which was bursting at the seams, greeted us bellowing his almighty, 'HO HO HO.'

'Hello Father Christmas you don't have to worry about giving me a present in the hospital this year because I'm going home. You can give my present to another boy or girl,' Chiara said excitedly.

We returned to hospital on the 26th as promised. A time I wish upon reflection, I had refused permission for surgery, because by then she appeared too healthy to have a blocked shunt. But what would I know, when I'm *only* the mother?

The procedure went ahead as planned only to discover the shunt was working, leading me to ask whether it was possible for shunts to have intermittent blockages, which clear on their own. The differing conclusion amongst doctors at the time was either there was no such thing or it was a definite possibility. Professor Simpson discharged us early the next morning.

\*\*\*

Chiara's third birthday, 11 July 1990, was supposed to be a celebration but she became ill and subsequently spent the second out of three birthdays in what had become our second home. Two out of three Easters and two out of three Christmases were spent with her in a hospital bed.

\*\*\*

Over the next six months we attended the Emergency Department numerous times with symptoms of shunt malfunction only to have her recover soon after arriving, running around as though nothing had happened. With her blood pressure, temperature and pupil reactions all normal, it made for a baffling and frustrating time for staff reliant on the results, to help determine if Chiara had a blockage. It seemed to me she was experiencing intermittent blockages.

I discussed the possibility with Mr Hanieh on his return but he wasn't convinced shunts would do that. Influenced by the fact it was happening so often, my mind was already made up but all I had to go on was my intuition, and what I was witnessing with Chiara. But again, only being a mother, what would I know?

I believed I had the shunts sussed and was now one step ahead. Rather than rush off to hospital too afraid to take the slightest chance, I'd observe her closely to see if she improved over the following hour. Providing she didn't deteriorate and frighten me I would make her comfortable, laying her down with head propped up to avoid choking if she were to vomit.

Instead of running around I would calmly organise things in readiness for a hospital stay. Not knowing whether we would be back home the same day or months later was always a concern, especially if I was in the middle of doing the washing. There were times I returned from a panicked emergency trip that had turned into a lengthy stay, only to discover mouldy clothes in the washing machine.

*** 

Chiara became a clingy child with separation issues, which was understandable after all she had suffered. I enlisted the help of a child psychologist who taught me skills to deal with her. Every morning, she had to be in the bathroom with me or she would scream at the door.

Dani was a phenomenal help, especially while she was living at home. I don't know how I would have managed those early years if not for her support. Without complaint she would jump out of bed in the middle of the night whenever Chiara took ill and nurse her on her lap in the car, while Chiara often vomited along the way. It wasn't much of a life for a young teenager when most school holidays were spent at the hospital, while her friends were enjoying whatever teenagers did when they didn't have a seriously ill sibling.

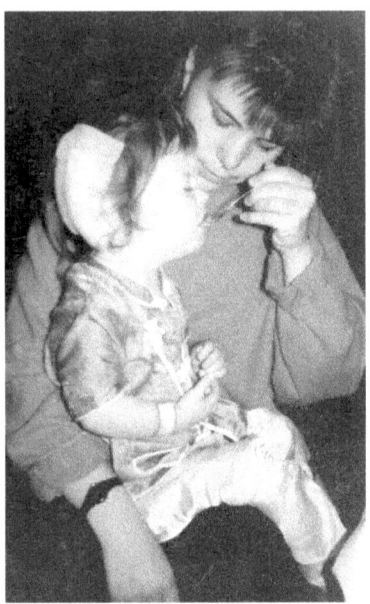

*Dani helps to feed Chiara*

Undergoing neurosurgery so often was having a devastating effect on Chiara's feeble body. Physiotherapy sessions weren't enjoyed so we did as much as we could at home. I purchased a swing set, trampoline and bikes anything to help build Chiara's muscles while pretending it was play time, trying to give her as normal a life as possible away from the hospital.

In early December 1990, when she didn't improve after presenting with her well known shunt symptoms of vomiting, irritability and sleepiness, Mr Hanieh discovered the 'bottom' shunt that was draining the cyst in her brain stem had blocked. Assured she wasn't in danger, with Christmas fast approaching he offered the choice as to whether I preferred the operation performed before or after Christmas.

At first I considered it best to wait, however reflecting on Chiara's history I soon changed my mind knowing if postponed, we risked another Christmas in hospital, so surgery was scheduled. On the 13th December the shunt was replaced to enable the cyst to continue to drain and we were home a couple of days later. With the latest admission behind us, we looked forward to a healthy, happy, and for Chiara, an exciting Christmas.

Eleven days later, on Christmas Eve, she began showing the typical subtle signs which were difficult to describe other than to say, she isn't right. A mother knows her child and identifies when there's something wrong. I chose to momentarily ignore it, I didn't want to know.

Not another Christmas in hospital surely? It was what we were supposed to be avoiding. Mentally drained, aware of the inevitable, I watched her closely to see what would transpire. We attended a party in the evening and she fell asleep on my lap which was unusual, as bedtime was an ongoing battle in our house. The only time she fell asleep early was when she was ill. I clung to the possibility it would prove to be an intermittent blockage and the impending drama wouldn't unfold. At 6am Christmas morning she awoke, excited to see what Father Christmas had brought her. While unwrapping presents she was delighted to notice a swing set through the window.

While swinging to and fro she kept asking, 'But how did Father Christmas fit this in his bag?' She started vomiting and it was painfully clear on presentation of all three symptoms the shunt had blocked. I took her to hospital but again soon after arriving, she improved. Spotting Father Christmas she ran towards him demanding to know how he fitted the swing set in his bag. By that time we had presented to the Emergency Department often enough the regular staff knew us and what to expect from Chiara so we were now prioritised as a matter of caution or urgency.

I was always relieved to see familiar faces and soon had favourites which meant I only had to approach the desk saying, 'we're back.' As it was Christmas Day it was agreed the shunt appeared to have cleared so it was safe to go home where we resumed the waiting game. We joined the rest of our family for lunch.

*One night when I went to check on Chiara, thinking she was asleep, I discovered her kneeling at the side of her bed, praying. I didn't realise she knew how to pray.*

\*\*\*

With Chiara unwell one minute, and running around the next, it continued to be a perplexing time. Mr Hanieh had witnessed these episodes often enough to acknowledge intermittent shunt blockages were indeed possible, and so too Professor Simpson. They didn't have any other explanation for her suddenly becoming well, after initially presenting very ill with all the symptoms of malfunction.

During the early hours of 26 December 1990 the vomiting and other symptoms started again. I had learnt to streamline time spent in the Emergency Department by ringing first to alert them to our impending arrival. Doing so allowed staff to have her medical records brought to the department and if necessary have a doctor on standby, which saved a great deal of time and stress in the waiting room.

Mr Hanieh was summoned from his sleep and without delay a scan revealed a blockage so she went back to theatre.

At three-and-a-half years old, undergoing neurosurgery for the tenth time, I questioned why she was having so much trouble. Mr Hanieh informed me it was common for a young child to undergo more shunt revisions than an older child or adult. He believed the revisions would lessen as she got older.

*\*\*\**

One of the doctors at the children's hospital who realised I wasn't leaving Chiara's side suggested I invest in a pager and I couldn't get to the shop quickly enough to buy one. It changed my life, giving me the confidence to leave her in hospital, or with my parents for short periods, secure in the knowledge as long as the pager remained silent, I didn't have to rush back.

Life instantly became slightly more bearable. That small technological device gave me a touch of freedom and some peace of mind that I hadn't known since the day she was born. Discharged from hospital a few days later, I carried Chiara down to my car. As soon as I placed her in the car seat it was evident the shunt had already blocked again but I decided to take her home hoping it would prove to be an intermittent blockage and clear. It was Saturday morning and as the day progressed rather than improve, by 4pm she became disoriented. I had waited too long.

This hadn't happened before, so I was particularly worried, scolding myself for taking her home and not straight back to Mr Hanieh when I first noticed she wasn't right, in the car. Not wanting to risk being sent home because she had only been discharged hours earlier and wanting to catch him before he left for the day, in desperation I rang Mr Hanieh's office.

Not surprisingly, he advised me to immediately revisit the hospital where he would meet us. I was already distraught and then met with an intern declaring, 'It can't possibly be the shunt it's too soon.' Thank God I rang Mr Hanieh first, as for Chiara, sadly, there's no such luxury as too soon. Mr Hanieh arrived, took one look at her and immediately arranged surgery.

A week later we were discharged but days later returned to again be met with the declaration, 'It can't be the shunt!' It's challenging to remain composed when I want to scream, it *is* the shunt. The intern proclaimed there was nothing wrong and said to take her home but I insisted he inform Mr Hanieh we were there. Reluctantly he agreed to admit her then retreated. As the hours passed, waiting anxiously in Fielders Ward for Mr Hanieh, I wondered why he was taking so long, unless he was in theatre.

We'd been through it numerous times so I knew what to expect. He was always quickly on the scene and if it weren't possible he would ring me. We were in a share room and as nurses were constantly attending the child in the next bed I was despairing because no-one was checking on Chiara as she continued to deteriorate.

By late afternoon when her left eye turned in towards her nose and she appeared dazed and lethargic I grabbed the first nurse I could find and begged her to call Mr Hanieh urgently. He soon appeared in the doorway inquiring as to how long we'd been there and why he hadn't been informed. I started to explain what happened, when he brushed past me scooped her up in his arms, instructing the nurse to ring the operating theatre to say he was on his way with Chiara.

His patient neglected too long, a normally placid Mr Hanieh was noticeably angry as he carried Chiara out the ward leaving me agonising over what we were facing, grateful for his swift actions. He wasn't waiting for an orderly to take her; there wasn't time. After the surgery he handed me a piece of paper and in his shy, quiet manner simply said, 'Here are my home and mobile phone numbers.'

A tremendous comfort to have them, I thanked him and assured him I would never abuse the gesture and only use his private numbers if absolutely necessary. Had I been listened to, Mr Hanieh could have planned the surgery, instead of having to swiftly act like he did, and Chiara wouldn't have ended up so very ill, and been left with a squint, often referred to as 'crossed' eyes. I was seething.

\*\*\*

If a shunt blockage is left too long, eyes can turn in as excess pressure builds in the brain. It was then that I understood why Mr Hanieh had told me it is best to have her at the hospital within two hours. As a consequence I was informed Chiara suffered third and sixth nerve palsy affecting her eyes.

Sometimes eyes can recover without intervention otherwise surgery can be performed to straighten them. Chiara wore an eye patch for many months alternating between the left and right eye each day to try to force them to straighten naturally while wearing glasses to help correct her eyesight. Surgery was performed at a later date to straighten her eyes.

\*\*\*

Not recovering as expected, a CAT scan revealed yet another blockage, so again back to theatre, and yet again a few days later. New Year's Eve 1990 we were still in hospital. I had planned a fund-raising night for the Queen Victoria Hospital months beforehand and with too many preparations still to take care of, I set about cancelling it. I made some phone calls and a couple of hours later, friends Judy and Sam arrived, casually informing me the pig-pen party was going ahead and all I had to do was arrive if at all possible.

By 3pm the day of the fund-raiser, with Chiara beginning to show signs of improvement, Mr Hanieh insisted I go out and enjoy the evening. I was surprised when he promised to look after her himself. When my mother arrived unexpectedly with her overnight bag in hand, the pair of them sent me out the door. It was just one of many occasions my mother arrived with a packed bag taking my place on a fold-up bed or chair so I could return home to my own bed, to try to sleep for a night.

Not only I but also my parents couldn't bear to think of their tiniest grandchild all alone in hospital. Some staff considered they were doing the parent a favour by not telling them what happened in their absence. However it becomes problematic when someone, usually a visitor to a neighbouring patient, exaggerates in the telling of what had occurred, which causes more stress than necessary. It's just one of the reasons I prefer to be there throughout, sleep or no sleep.

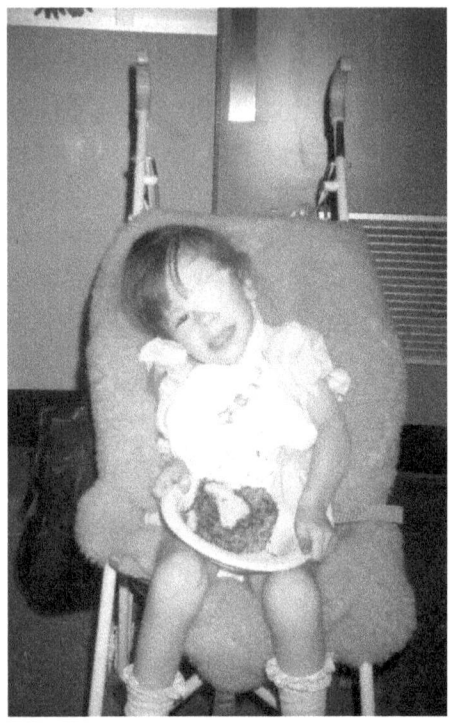

*Chiara wearing her eye patch briefly shows signs of improvement and asks for a lamington*

Checking in with the hospital before leaving home, I was ordered to stop worrying and have some fun. Chiara asked for a lamington at tea time so it appeared she was much better. The night I didn't think would happen was a success thanks to the generosity of the Wills family who donated the pig-pen on their property for our party and also to Tony the Disc Jockey who kindly donated his services, helping to raise a few more dollars.

# *One step forward two steps back*

New Year's Day 1991, Chiara was back in theatre. It marked the beginning of our worst year. A CAT scan on January 3 revealed enlarged ventricles in the brain but instead of being blocked, the shunt was too long. Mr Hanieh reduced the length in the operating theatre, and placed it back into the ventricle. A Central Venous Catheter (CVC) was inserted to make it easier to put intravenous drips in, as most of her veins were collapsing and no longer viable. Chiara's body was a mass of tiny dots testament to the hundreds of butterfly needles and drips inserted into her veins since the day she was born.

January 11 saw another revision and after spending six weeks in hospital Chiara had recovered enough to go home. Within a week we were back to see Mr Hanieh. Her life had become one step forward and two steps back. The frequent rounds of gruelling neurosurgery were taking their toll. No longer able to walk, talk, sit up, crawl or even perform the most menial of tasks, my determined young daughter, weighing a mere ten kilograms, had become totally dependent on me.

Intensive physiotherapy had begun but whether she would recover and develop to her full potential was an unknown factor, given the shunts were causing havoc. An urgent scan revealed a blockage that resulted in surgery, and more again a couple of days later. Chiara was

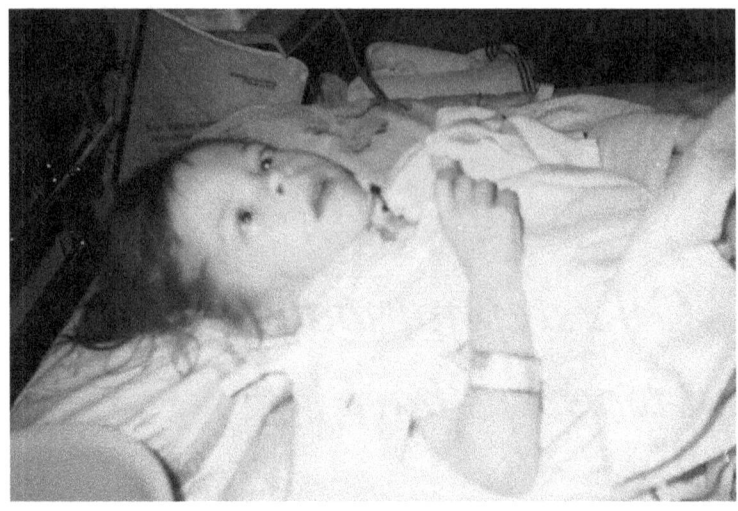
*Chiara age 4yrs*

fighting a huge battle to survive and through it all I continued to be physically and mentally drained, utterly distraught, watching helplessly as Chiara battled on. We were struggling to grasp why the shunts kept blocking.

Mr Hanieh eventually discovered Chiara was producing a rare form of brain debris never seen or heard of before. The debris was breaking down causing constant blockages. Her perilous condition left me traumatised. I wondered if her brain was rejecting the shunts. I questioned both Mr Hanieh and Professor Simpson but they weren't able to answer me, except to say they had to keep an open mind, unsure of exactly what they were dealing with. The next day they came to talk to me, together. My heart sank, knowing for them to approach as a team, meant something significant.

They had been devising a plan to perform a decompression of Chiara's skull. They hoped it would allow more time between blockages and revisions while they worked on the cause of the debris, and how to stop it. I did my best to remain calm hoping to disguise my horror, grateful they hadn't given up and were desperate to help. Trusting them implicitly, and without any other options, I agreed.

The procedure involved removing approximately a one inch (two centimetre) square piece at the base of her skull to allow more room as pressure built up inside her head, thus buying time between surgeries. Resolving not to delay any longer, surgery was performed on February 26, marking the beginning of yet another nightmare.

The whispering lady was back. 'Trust in God Helen, trust in God.' To trust in God was exasperating when all I could think of was, 'suffer the little children.' The soft reassuring whisper continued throughout the agony, the anguish and the suffering. Whenever I was overcome with terror heading into the depths of despair, an unexplained comforting sensation would accompany each whisper.

Chiara didn't recover as well as hoped. She was gravely ill and in undeniable agony. Painkillers had been kept to a minimum so as not to mask any neurological symptoms. On reflection, I should have taken a risk and insisted she be kept completely pain free. When a child can yell and scream you can gauge how much pain they are in but when too weak and ill to cry it's difficult to assess the extent of their pain.

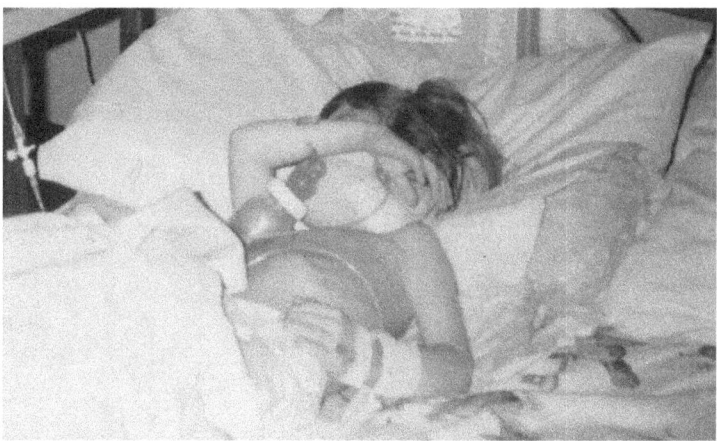

*Surgeries are taking their toll*

Willing her to survive and existing in zombie mode feeling totally broken, I wasn't in any condition to support Chiara, and as the tears flowed all I could do was lie on her bed, and hold her. Regardless of how often she took ill it didn't get any easier. I would often sit in my car, a store-room or stairwell, and bawl my eyes out away from everyone. No words are powerful enough to adequately describe the effect a critically ill child has on a parent.

Chiara continued to be unresponsive, and by Saturday night I asked for Mr Hanieh to be contacted. Her breathing was shallow and she looked frightfully ill. When he arrived, with a look of despair he sent her straight into Intensive Care. Four days later the Head of the Intensive Care Unit came to tell me he was sending her back to the ward. He was apologetic saying there wasn't anything more medically he or his team could do. It was horrific hearing his words, watching her again fight for life, without any explanation why she was critically ill, and now without further medical help. All anyone could do was watch and pray.

# *Special kisses*

The following day I met Dr Chris in the corridor. At the time he was a neurosurgery registrar. I told him I believed Chiara's brain was rejecting the shunts, that she was unresponsive, barely alive, hardly eating and all she could manage to do was to sleep or stare. I told him I thought she was giving up the battle. Dr Chris was visibly moved and saddened to hear what we were grappling with. He said he wished he knew what to say, or do, that could help.

Back in Chiara's room I deliberated on what, if anything, I could buy to excite her enough to rouse a response. I desperately wanted my little girl to snap out of the state she was in, to look at me, and talk to me, to just show some sign of improvement but I didn't know how to make it happen. I started thinking about all the things and the people she loved, and her favourite toys. Then it hit me. Humphrey Bear! When she was well enough, Chiara loved watching 'Here's Humphrey' on television every morning. I contacted Rae Craddock, the then Queen Victoria Hospital Public Relations Officer and asked if she could contact Channel Nine to get Humphrey to visit the hospital. 'Helen it's the least I can do, consider it done,' came the reply.

Humphrey appeared unannounced the next day. As he gently stroked Chiara's arm, with almost the entire ward looking on, she started to blink trying to open her eyes. She was so fragile it was a major effort to focus on what was in front of her. For the first time in weeks she strained to speak, 'It's Humphrey, the *real* Humphrey!' Tears flowed as staff and visitors were visibly moved and even Humphrey was seen to wipe a tear from his eye.

*Humphrey Bear, my mother and Chiara 1991*

That bear accomplished more in a few moments than medicine and technology achieved in weeks. Chiara's improvement was immediate and dramatic, and as Humphrey moved in closer she managed to kiss him on the nose. Back from the brink, her speech was so severely affected a therapist was enlisted to help but at least she was trying to talk. They say God works in mysterious ways; well, Humphrey Bear worked a miracle that day.

On hearing the news Dr Chris didn't hesitate to visit. Arriving at her bedside he said 'Chiara, you have to get better now because I'm getting married soon. I want you to come to the church on my wedding day and give me a kiss.' Chiara smiled signalling she understood. She adored Dr Chris and would love to see him get married. The wedding became an incentive for any time she looked like slipping backwards.

The day arrived and although barely able to speak, Chiara managed to ask Mr Hanieh to lift her up out of her bed. She then managed to ask if he'd let her go and give Dr Chris a kiss on his wedding day.

'Of course you can Chiara. You can go and mum can bring you back when you're ready. Go and have some time away from the hospital and give Dr Chris that kiss.'

*Mr Hanieh tells Chiara she can go to a wedding*

Dressed in one of her prettiest dresses we headed off. Weighing only ten kilograms - approximately twenty two pounds - she was light to carry. Her scrawny, floppy body sat slumped in the car seat. So delicate and pitifully frail she wasn't going to disappoint Dr Chris. The last time she had been in the car, she was looking out the window, chatting and admiring the scenery but now she couldn't even hold her head up. Even so, she was happy to be going to see Dr Chris and his pretty bride. Driving to the chapel, typically, Chiara kept asking, 'Are we there yet, Mummy?'

Half an hour passed before I could finally say, 'Yes darling we're here. I'm going to park the car and we'll go and find Dr Chris so you can give him that kiss you promised.'

I carried her towards the chapel looking around at all the guests but I couldn't see Dr Chris. I then realised he would be inside with his groomsmen. I contemplated what to do as Chiara wasn't well enough to wait until after the service. I knew that as the bride hadn't arrived, we had time to do what we had gone there for but I had to move quickly if Dr Chris was going to get his kiss.

Everyone in the chapel was talking quietly and Dr Chris was standing near the altar. We set off down the aisle with Chiara's skinny legs protruding from her dress and her heavily bandaged head resting on my shoulder. With the guests busily chatting I didn't think they would take any notice of us but then silence befell each pew we passed. Oh no! What had I done? It wasn't the right thing to do, it was rude but it was too late.

With two pews to go Dr Chris sensed something was happening behind his back. His face lit up as he slowly turned, with a chapel full of now-silent guests looking on in awe. He held his arms out and gently lifted Chiara from me holding her flimsy body as she happily gave him the kiss she had promised. A gasp swept through the congregation. I then carried a very contented little girl to the back of the chapel to find a seat. The bride arrived looking radiant in her elegant wedding gown.

Chiara was very excited and began chatting. She hadn't spoken so many words in weeks and although I couldn't understand her, I had to ask her to be quiet. Halfway through the service she began to wane; we had to get back to the hospital. I waited for an appropriate time and we quickly made our exit. The special day had been too much for Chiara but Dr Chris was given his kiss, with Chiara deliriously happy she was able to do so.

# *Complications continue*

In 1987, the year Chiara was born, the Royal Adelaide Hospital was fortunate to have the Commonwealth Government purchase Adelaide's first public Magnetic Resonance Imaging Scanner (referred to as an MRI scanner). Until the day Mr Hanieh booked Chiara's first MRI scan I hadn't heard of such a machine. It was explained that the CAT scanner at the Women's and Children's Hospital was 'useful' but the MRI would leave little doubt as to what was wrong.

With the scan booked, the arrangements were explained to me. A nurse, anaesthetist and I would travel across town in an ambulance with Chiara, where she would undergo the MRI under a general anaesthetic. It can be a frightening experience, especially for a young child, and it is critical to remain completely still.

At the time there was an eight week waiting list but as Chiara was barely conscious and in need of an urgent scan she *only* had to wait ten days. It was incomprehensible that any child should have to wait, considering when booking MRI scans, one can be talking life and death situations.

While awaiting her scan, Chiara's condition deteriorated, so Mr Hanieh was forced to perform emergency surgery not knowing exactly what he was dealing with. Discovering a cyst was again building up all he could do was replace the shunt and hope for the best. Chiara recovered slightly and fortunately Mr Hanieh didn't cancel the MRI appointment.

When the day arrived for the MRI we were transported across to the Royal Adelaide Hospital by ambulance, and as per protocol, an anaesthetist and nurse travelled with us. Once the scan was complete, we returned to Fielder's Ward to wait for the radiologist from the Women's and Children's Hospital to travel to the Royal Adelaide Hospital, read the scan and then return the report back to Mr Hanieh.

The MRI scan revealed a second cyst at the base of Chiara's brain. It was situated alongside the original cyst and Mr Hanieh was able to break the wall separating them, combining them into one which couldn't be removed. It was explained to me that it was like a bubble, and from time to time it can multiply, similar to the effect you get when blowing bubbles.

Shunt blockages and surgeries continued as Chiara resumed a second-by-second existence with life nearly unbearable for us all. The hospital became our permanent home.

As Easter approached, Chiara was lying on pillows on my lap. I reflected on the number of times over the years, I had gone away for the Easter break, often taking Dani camping with a group of friends. I longed for Chiara to stay well long enough so I could take her on holidays too. Without complaint Dani spent most school holidays, Easters and special occasions at the hospital.

*** 

We were sitting by Chiara's cot one afternoon when Dani decided to go for a walk to the kiosk to buy a drink. Minutes later she came running back petrified.

'Dani, what's wrong?'

'Mum, there's hundreds of bikies out there. You should see them they're really scary. What do they want? What will we do if they all come in here?'

'Dani calm down. They're not here to hurt anyone, they visit every year. Haven't you seen them in here before?'

'No. What do they want? Why are they here?'

'Every year at Christmas they have a toy run and they bring the toys here to the kids and at Easter they bring Easter eggs. They won't hurt you, don't be silly and go and get your drink.'

'No way! I'm not going anywhere until they leave.' Poor terrified Dani wasn't leaving my side with a hospital full of 'ferocious' looking bikers.

\*\*\*

During April 1991, Chiara, dangerously ill with a raging temperature, was diagnosed with pneumonia. To further complicate matters, her cerebral spinal fluid (CSF) once again, also became infected. An exhausted team of microbiologists including the brilliant Dr Goldwater were working continuously, baffled as to what was going on with her.

After a long wait, Dr Goldwater arrived to deliver the devastating news of his findings. The deadly spinal fluid infection was identified as Pseudomonas. I was informed that it is a revolting slimy green microorganism that exists in a number of places, such as shower heads, and can become airborne. It sometimes attacks when a person is very ill rendering them powerless to fight its invasion.

Chiara, bed-ridden in hospital for so long, was thought to have swallowed the bug. Mr Hanieh declared war on the evil beast. Each time he replaced an infected shunt the Pseudomonas invaded the new one, resulting in multiple neurosurgical shunt revisions.

Thursday 25 April, Anzac Day, emotionally exhausted I deliberated on what the day would bring and how it would end, optimistically hoping it would be the day Mr Hanieh successfully beat the bug. Instead, he took Chiara back to theatre. Each time she went into surgery I was permitted into a side room to hold her, while she was anaesthetised with the 'smelly gas' she hated so much. I hated seeing her upset and having to leave her. The care and compassion, dignity and respect shown to us by ward and theatre staff was always reassuring, forever ready with a box of tissues for me.

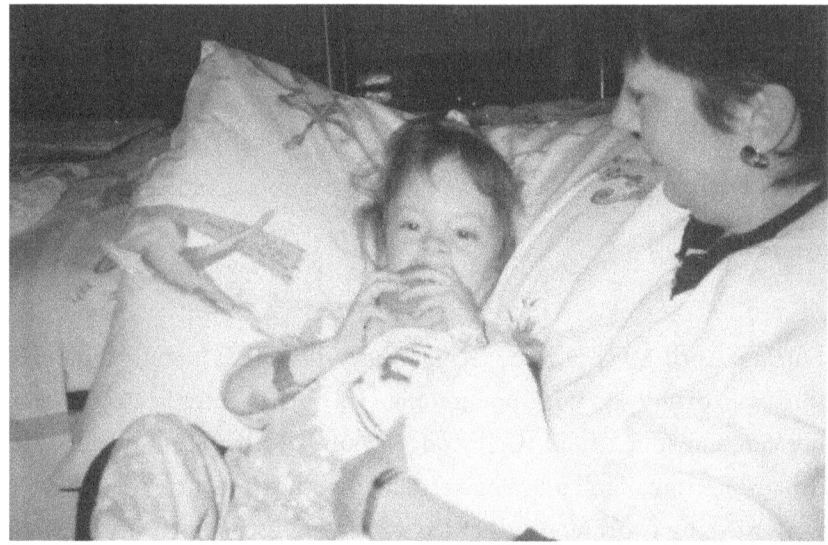

*Chiara and Helen*

*Easter 1991 on the Play deck at the Women's and Children's Hospital Aged 4yrs*

Friday 26 April another bug-infected shunt revision. Lack of sleep added to the trauma. I began to drag myself through each day wanting to collapse somewhere, anywhere. I hadn't been home for weeks and couldn't remember the last time I slept in a bed. I was kindly offered a room in the nurses' quarters but I declined as it was too far away from Chiara.

Staff from the Intensive Care Unit, concerned for my welfare, surprised me when they offered me a lovely motel-type room that was attached to the unit. I didn't even know it existed, and I felt like I had won a lottery. Decorated in soft pastel shades it became a tranquil retreat for me in the late evenings, and was close to Chiara. When given the room I was told I would lose it if a country child arrived as it would be offered to the parents.

As I was living in the hospital without anywhere to sleep I was grateful and felt privileged to have the room for however long I was permitted to. At times the staff in Fielders ward allowed me to sleep on a fold-up bed in their 'handover' room while Chiara was in Intensive Care, not that I slept but it was much appreciated just to have somewhere to rest close by whenever she was stable.

Chiara was again barely responsive other than to hold my hand tightly, relaying a silent message, 'Please don't leave me mummy.' Not permitted access to the 'motel' room every night, I was battling to exist without sleep but knowing Dani was being well cared for by my parents, I refused to go home. There were many times I wandered aimlessly, back and forth along the wide, lengthy corridor between Intensive Care and Fielders ward, tears streaming down my face, hoping a bed would appear for me to get some much-needed sleep.

There were many times I thought I couldn't go on, scared I would collapse on the floor and embarrass myself. Empty hospital beds near Chiara became an enormous temptation and I could easily have hijacked one. Existing on very little sleep, sitting in a chair next to her day and night, it was hard trying to absorb everything I was being told by her doctors, while my brain was a complete fuzz and life a blur.

Intensive Care was the best place for her but understandably there wasn't anywhere for a parent to sleep other than in a chair. On the wards there were some recliner chairs for parents to rest in but there weren't always enough for everyone. After many years, much appreciated sofa beds were introduced to the hospital making life a little easier for exhausted parents.

Saturday April 27 1991, was to become the worst day of my life. Chiara surprised me by appearing to be alert and happy when she awoke. She was talking and asked to have the television turned on. Relieved, I flicked through the stations to find a show suitable for her to watch. Trevor, my younger brother, was on his way from Melbourne and older brother Greg was bringing my mother and Dani in to visit. I was pleased Chiara was well enough to see them all. Lying on the bed she turned to look at me and I noticed she was waning. As the subtle symptoms grew more intense I calmly informed the nurse assigned to her care that I was concerned but she couldn't see the change.

The hours passed and I became increasingly worried. I spoke to Dr Matthews who agreed to immediately assess her but he too was unable to identify the subtle difference in her demeanour. Chiara wasn't right but frustratingly, as far as the staff were concerned all medical observations appeared normal. Dr Matthews tried his best to reassure me, promising to keep a very close eye on her but I recognised disaster was looming, and it wouldn't be long before it became evident to those caring for her.

Aware the team was conscious of my fears, I quickly ran downstairs to buy some lunch, mindful once all hell broke loose, I wouldn't feel like eating. Some people eat more under duress, while I can't when my stomach's churning with anxiety. Whatever was going on in the outside world was irrelevant, and with the chronic lack of sleep and unable to afford any decent hospital canteen food, I struggled to get through each day.

Most of my meals consisted of buttered rolls as I found them to be filling, and I could buy two for less than a dollar but that day I knew I would need a bit more sustenance, so I bought a salad sandwich and ate it on the way back to Chiara. Less than fifteen minutes had lapsed but when I walked into the room Dr Matthews and his team had all gathered around her.

Rushing towards her I gasped, 'Oh no Dr Matthews what's happened, she's grey!'

'Helen you've been telling us all morning she's not right, you're simply never wrong. We should've taken more notice of your concerns. I'm so sorry.' Dr Matthews always trusted my intuition and ability to recognise the subtle symptoms but couldn't act until medical symptoms became obvious in order to know exactly what he was dealing with, and not just my intuition. Chiara's 'observations' suddenly started going berserk leaving no doubt the Pseudomonas was again determined to reign supreme.

The team moved aside to allow me access to Chiara, while Dr Matthews went to the desk to urgently ring Mr Hanieh. I hold Intensive Care doctors and nursing staff in the highest regard and never blame anyone for not identifying her subtle symptoms. How can I, when it is only my intuition that recognises when trouble looms? I can't explain it. I am her mother and the only person in tune with her subtle changes. All I have ever asked is that medical and nursing staff listen to a mother's concerns, even if the child appears well.

Tears flooding my face and clothes, I could barely see as I slumped sobbing onto Chiara's bed. Resembling a flimsy rag doll, I gently lifted her into my arms. Tenderly holding her against my chest, slowly and carefully rocking backwards and forwards, my precious miracle girl was dying. Overcome with grief I questioned whether she had the strength to continue fighting the hideous monster.

Unconscious, her head on my shoulder while carefully supported by my right hand, her tiny bottom cradled in my left, I continued to rock gently, my tears saturating her hair. The morning had been restful with the bluest of skies, fluffy clouds and golden sunbeams dancing through the window and she appeared to be doing well. Inconceivably her scrawny body was being ravaged by the out-of-control beast, hell bent on demanding she succumb to its overwhelming oppressive power. The sterile room was full of the best available lifesaving equipment that Chiara had pushed to its limit, and rendered useless.

Begging her not to die, a sudden sense of selfishness engulfed me. I didn't have the right to expect her to live if she wanted to give up her courageous battle. Dr Matthews re-entered the room saying Mr Hanieh wished to speak to me on the phone. I walked towards the desk and with the phone in hand barely managed to speak. 'Hello' was all I could say and Mr Hanieh asked, 'Helen how do you think Chiara is?' Choking on tears, 'Oh Mr Hanieh I'm so scared. I've never seen her look like this, she's very sick.'

'I'll order a scan immediately and if it reveals another blocked shunt, I'll come in and take her to theatre. I'll wait by the phone for the results.' I wanted to beg him to come straight in.

Whimpering, I returned to Chiara's bedside. Trying to stabilise her to prepare for the scan proved to be a dire effort. Sitting on the bed, I again carefully lifted her into my arms.

Grief stricken, drowning in a flood of tears, I noticed my family members stopped in the doorway. Shocked at what was obviously going on, not a word was spoken. They locked their arms around us, they too were crying. Chiara was barely alive, fighting a seemingly impossible battle. We were losing her.

Word came from the radiologist to say the CAT scanner was ready and theatre prepared. As the team wheeled her out on her bed, I was crushed with despair as a whisper filtered through the staff, '*Only a miracle can save her now.*' Heartbroken, terrified and completely shattered that my baby couldn't possibly survive, I heard 'Trust in God Helen, trust in God.' The voice was back but it made me angry. Whose voice was it? How could I trust in God when my baby was cruelly suffering? The grief unbearable, I was desperate for another miracle. Sitting with my family, head in my hands quietly sobbing, something made me look up.

Through the tears I could scarcely make out a figure standing silently in the doorway. It was Mr Hanieh. He couldn't stay home waiting by the phone knowing we were in trouble. Having him there brought immense relief, not only to me but to my family and the staff. That caring, compassionate man was my sanity. Never for as long as I live will I forget his shattered look as he gazed, broken-hearted at Chiara as she was wheeled past him. He looked at me, before he turned and followed behind her.

The CAT scan resulted in her being whisked into theatre. I wasn't permitted to go as every second was crucial so I waited with my family. Everyone, including the staff were visibly affected by the events leading up to that moment. We were all family in the Intensive Care Unit and everyone felt the sorrow. Chiara won many hearts and the support my family and I received was overwhelming, yet I felt alone. Only a mother who had experienced such trauma would know the torture searing through my veins.

Dealing with our grief in silence, we passed the hours sitting in or pacing the waiting area, while other family members awaited news at home. Mentally going through the motions of how I was going to deal with losing her, I was shaking when Mr Hanieh appeared. 'It's an absolute miracle Helen, I was really worried and didn't think she'd come through this time but incredibly she's now out of danger; she hasn't given up.' The overwhelming relief was immeasurable. Words cannot explain how I felt hearing that news. We made it through the next day, Sunday but by 1am Monday morning Mr Hanieh was beckoned from his bed, and Chiara's shunt revised yet again.

Tuesday 30th at 3am the Pseudomonas was wreaking havoc. Determining the peritoneal (stomach) cavity needed a break from the shunt, Mr Hanieh inserted a ventricular atrium shunt, which meant the cysts and fourth ventricle were simultaneously flowing to the atrium (chamber) of her heart, instead of the peritoneal cavity. The worry of what it would do to her heart was of paramount concern to me but Mr Hanieh's reassurances lay in the fact that initially it was the way all shunts were inserted.

# *My consolation*

May 6 1991, Chiara was discharged from Intensive Care and returned to Fielders ward. A cocktail of antibiotics pumped through her veins eventually helped to combat the Pseudomonas ravaging her body but Chiara remained desperately ill.

A mother visiting her young daughter in the bed next to us approached me and said, 'I don't know how you cope.' I was aghast. Her ten-year-old daughter had the day before, been diagnosed with Cancer and there she stood wondering how *I* cope. Her reasoning was she and her husband knew what was wrong with their daughter and consequently what they may have to prepare for, whereas Chiara was barely conscious without a prognosis. I coped because I knew there were many worse off than us and I still had my little girl.

My strength and consolation had been gained from watching a treasured friend devastated by the sudden loss of his adorable seven-year-old son after suffering an asthma attack, ten years before Chiara was born. I was completely shattered and still feel the grief knowing there can be nothing worse than losing a child. During my time spent in the hospital I witnessed families dealing with children with challenges, illnesses and syndromes far worse than Chiara's, with some caring for multiple chronically ill children.

Growing up witnessing the continuous battles one particular family bravely endured, gave me a valuable insight while very young into how confronting and traumatic life could be. Those remarkable parents without question or protest found the strength and stamina to deal with their chronically ill children while I've only had to deal with one. The harsh reality is, our lives could be so very much worse, I know because I have seen it. At least in between surgeries and hospital trips when Chiara is stable we get to pretend we live a normal life.

## Free wheel…ing

May 13 1991, we were back in Intensive Care after another complex shunt revision. The following day with my mother on duty and Chiara stable, I went home to do some washing and get some fresh air, expecting to be away for approximately two hours. With permission from the security guard I had been permitted to park in the old underground car-park at the hospital, a courtesy not normally extended to visitors. I think he felt sorry for me watching me driving around and around, constantly searching for carparks.

As soon as I'd finished the washing and packed fresh clothes I was on my way back to the hospital; my brief time away, over too soon. Driving along the road enjoying the warm sunshine, I watched in horror out the corner of my eye, as a wheel flew high up in the sky, ironically over the top of a hospital carpark. I watched the wheel, seemingly in slow motion, with visions of a total disaster, when I noticed people standing talking while holding a baby capsule. The wheel crashed down onto the bonnet of a small sedan. Luckily the noise alerted the people to the fact they were standing right in the path of an out-of-control wheel.

I slowed to find a carpark and suddenly my car dropped on one side. I froze. I was responsible for that dangerous flying chunk. Had it not happened to me I would never have believed it possible to lose a wheel and not know. I rushed towards the people gathered around the damaged car and meekly asked, 'Is anyone hurt?'

'Is this your wheel lady?'

'Yes it is I'm so sorry I can't believe this happened.'

'Boy, are *you* lucky, you should go and buy yourself a lottery ticket.'

'Lucky! How can you say I'm lucky? Look at this mess. Look at this car. Someone could've been killed.'

'Hey yeah but look lady we weren't, and look what's parked behind it.'

'Oh my God! A Mercedes!'

'Aren't you lucky you only wrote off the Galant and not the Merc?'

Feeling despondent, 'I guess so. I don't suppose any of you know who owns the Galant?'

'I think you may find the owner in the Radiology Department. I suggest you start there.'

'Thank you. I'm so grateful no-one was hurt and that I have comprehensive insurance to cover the damage.' A nervous wreck, I found the X-ray Department and was well aware of the time ticking away. I wanted to get back to Chiara. 'Excuse me, does anyone here own the beige Galant in the carpark?'

'Yes I do. Why?' Came a reply from behind the desk. 'I'm so sorry but I've just written it off. The back wheel came off my car and went flying through the air. It chose your car to plough through. If it's any consolation, I'm insured. Is there anything I can do for you now?'

'No just leave your details I'll go out and have a look at the damage.'

She seemed remarkably calm for someone who had just lost her transport. I then contacted Neil, my trusty mechanic and long-time friend. When he answered the phone I simply said, 'Help!'

'Helen, what's happened? Where are you?'

'A wheel flew off my car and totally demolished someone else's car. Can you please come and help me? I don't know what to do and Chiara is in hospital, I need to get back to her.'

'I'm on my way,' Neil said. Soon he arrived with his mate Dave, and as they pulled up I could hear them laughing. I wasn't impressed.

'Look at this mess you two. What's so funny? Someone could've been killed.'

'Oh Helen lighten up. We're laughing because this could only happen to *you*.'

They walked off up the road returning a short time later with Neil holding the four wheel nuts in his hands. 'Helen the fact we found all four nuts in the one place tends to make us think your car wheel was tampered with. If the wheel had worked its way loose over a period of time, the nuts would've been scattered all around Adelaide.'

When I reported the accident to Police they agreed the car was probably tampered with while parked in the underground carpark. I left the scene of the crime, wheel firmly in place, promising to ring the car owner with the insurance details. Two days later I rang to inform her, my insurance had inadvertently lapsed and apologised profusely while wondering what else could go wrong.

I had never been without comprehensive insurance since owning my first car but thankfully, she had her own cover and I didn't have to pay anything. Three years later Dr O'Loughlin sent me to the same hospital for an ultrasound. Thumbing through a magazine while awaiting my name to be called I heard a voice ask, 'Are you Chiara's mum?'

'Yes I am. I'm sorry, do I know you? How do you know Chiara?'

'Yes you do know me. You wrote my car off, remember?'

Wanting to shrivel up in disgrace I asked how she recognised me after such a long time and why she asked if I was Chiara's mum. 'I've been following you and Chiara's story through the media. I recognised you on TV soon after that accident and then in the newspapers. I've been interested in how you're both going ever since. Mr Hanieh was my neurosurgeon too!'

# *Jason*

After spending almost five months in hospital, and in and out of surgery, Chiara and I were finally home on May 18 but four days later she was undergoing her 28th shunt revision. We were home again on May 24. After many months of hospitalisation and surgeries she was still totally dependent on me. Chiara had lost so much weight that apart from making nutritious meals for her I also made what I called my wiz bang milkshakes of full cream milk, ice-cream, cream, yoghurt, egg, fruit; anything that would help put weight on her.

Soon after arriving home from the hospital, Chiara dragged herself down the long passageway to her bedroom. Nestling in amongst the toys she began chattering while Dani and I, preparing a meal in the kitchen, looked at each other bewildered. Who was she talking to? Dani and I crept toward Chiara's room. Even though she still struggled with her speech, she was deep in conversation but with whom? 'Chiara who are you talking to?' I asked expecting her to reply 'my doll' or 'my teddy.' With obscure baby like speech, 'I'm talking to J%#&n.'

'Who? Who are you talking to?'

'J%#&n.'

'Chiara I can't understand you. Who are you talking to?

'J…a…son'

'Jason. Who's Jason?' Dani and I asked simultaneously.

'You know, Jason. He's my friend and he's looking after me.'

'I can't see Jason, where is he hiding.'

'Up there,' was her reply.

'Where up there?'

'He's up there in Heaven with Jesus in the sky. He talks to me and he's looking after me.'

I went numb. She didn't know anyone called Jason but Dani and I did. Enjoying a much treasured friendship with his father, I was privileged to know and love Jason while sharing an all too brief part of his short life. Jason was the little seven year old boy who passed away during an asthma attack, ten years before Chiara was born.

Jason had been Dani's playmate, and my much cherished little friend but in an instant he was gone without the chance to say goodbye. Chiara's conversations with Jason continued throughout that horrendous period of 1991. Each time we returned home she crawled down to her room to talk to him, telling me Jason liked to sit in the rocking chair next to her bed.

*Chiara in her rocking chair that she said Jason liked to sit in*

A few times when Chiara stayed at my parent's home she told them Jason was there. One morning she awoke looking around the room. 'Chiara what's wrong?' my mother asked.

'He fibbed to me Nan,' said Chiara.

'Who fibbed to you darling?'

'Jason did. Jason fibbed to me Nan. He was here last night when I couldn't sleep cos of my headache and he said he'd stay but now he's gone. He promised me and I'm really cross with him. I thought he'd be here when I woke up.' On another occasion while staying at their house Chiara slept on a fold-up bed in my parent's room as she wasn't well and my mother wanted her close. To help ease Chiara's headache my mother went to get a wet face washer to put on her forehead.

'Nan! Didn't you *see* Jason?'

'No darling I didn't see Jason where is he?'

'Oh Nan you must've seen him you just walked straight *through* him, he was standing by the bed.'

Approximately a month later Chiara pulled out all the photo albums from the bottom shelf of our bookcase. I left her sitting on the lounge room floor looking through them and went into the kitchen while Dani was in her bedroom. Suddenly Chiara called out, 'Look mum see, here he is. I told you, you *know* him!'

'Here's *who* darling, who do I know?'

'Come here quick, he's here, here's Jason!'

Dani heard her call out, came into the kitchen looked at me then we walked into the lounge room.

'Chiara what do you mean 'here's Jason?'

'Look, here's a photo of him. You've got his photo in here. That's Jason, that's my friend. See! I told you, you know him.'

Dani and I were dumbfounded. I only had one photo of Jason taken just before he died. We didn't need proof that Chiara was having 'visions' and seeing Jason but we now had it anyway. I took comfort in the belief he had taken on the role of her Guardian Angel, and I am confident he will always look after her.

# *The nightmare continues*

In 1991 Chiara began exhibiting the seizures that I had been warned about, when she was born. A paediatric neurologist we consulted couldn't find a cause or explanation and deemed it probable the cyst at the base of her brain was the cause. She was prescribed Carbamazepine otherwise known as Tegretol but when that medication failed he prescribed Phenobarbitone, and the seizures were brought under control.

June 24 1991, a month after returning home from hospital we were due back to see Mr Hanieh. Chiara was very excited to be visiting her special friend. As we neared the hospital I sensed she wasn't right. She had been chirpy and excited but was now quiet and pale. The scenario was all too familiar but as we were seeing Mr Hanieh anyway, I chose to ignore it. There was always a faint hope it would prove to be an intermittent blockage.

We joined Mr Hanieh and his team in the Neurosurgery Department. They were all shaking their heads, commenting on how healthy Chiara looked, and how well she was progressing. I quietly mentioned to Mr Hanieh that I didn't think she was very well but that she'd been fine when we left home. Without warning the vomiting started and an air of disbelief filled the room.

The abrupt onset of the vomiting was a normal pattern and it was the best thing that could've happened right in front of the neurosurgical team, who thought she looked very healthy. I finally had proof of what I had been saying all along; there aren't any real warnings just subtle changes.

Mr Hanieh aware of Chiara's ability to change his plans in a split second ordered an urgent CAT scan which revealed a blocked shunt. I thought it strange he allowed us to go home. My gut feeling was that he wasn't telling me everything, other than he booked an MRI scan for July 9. Something wasn't right but he wasn't saying.

On July 10, my mother's sixty-fifth birthday and the day before Chiara's fourth birthday, the results from the MRI scan revealed the cyst at the base of her brain had broken down into three cysts. I understood then why Mr Hanieh didn't tell me what he suspected. He had deemed it safe to postpone surgery until the following week so Chiara could enjoy the birthday celebrations.

Surgery was performed on the cysts on July 18. Shunt revisions usually took approximately one and a half hours but that procedure took a total of six hours. The time passed slowly. I was upset because it hadn't ever taken that long and was convinced something must have gone wrong. Mr Hanieh finally emerged from theatre. I don't know who was more exhausted, him or me. I questioned why it took six hours and in his quiet, shy manner he replied, 'Was it that long? I didn't know.' Smiling at me he said, 'I don't look at the clock.'

Later in the day with my mother and Dani at Chiara's bedside, I left for a short drive through the countryside. Into the cassette player went my theme song, *You'll Never Walk Alone* by Gerry and the Pacemakers. That song blaring through the speakers had helped my sanity many times.

Chiara improved slowly but she was still too weak to stand or sit and was bored lying in bed all day. I amazed myself at my ingenuity transforming a child's pedal car that I found in the hospital playroom, into a mobile bed for her. Staff were intrigued as I lay her on a pillow on top of the car with drip stand attached to the back, and pushed her along. Chiara enjoyed the grand tour, able to go in and out of lifts, along corridors, down to the kiosk and all around the hospital.

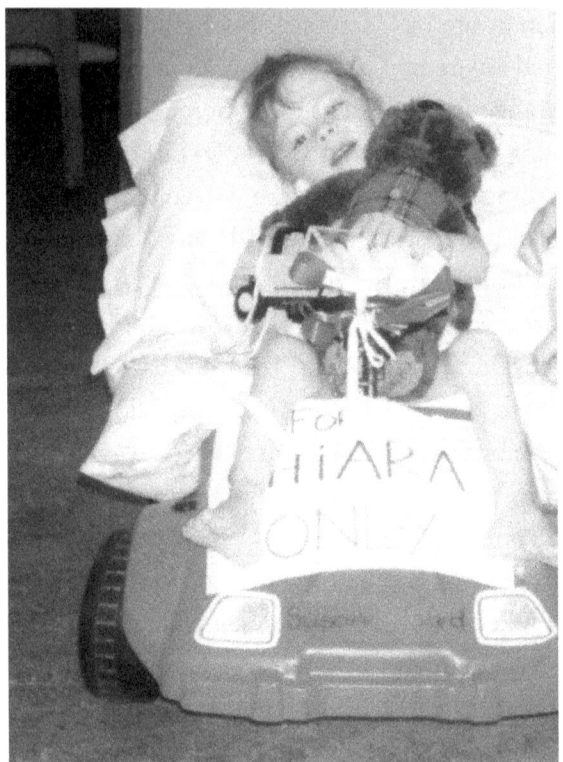

*Chiara loved the freedom of the pedal car*

She loved the freedom that car brought her, and for as long as she was small enough to fit on it, the car became part of our hospital routine. It never failed to put a smile on all the faces we saw along the way as we toured the hospital. The nurses even put her name on it. I wished children's wheelchairs were made to look like little cars with steering wheels and horns.

Following her latest round of surgery, Chiara declared the only person permitted to remove her sutures from then on was Mr Hanieh. One morning while discussing shunt problems with him and his team,

I accidentally called him 'Mr Shunt.' There was hysterics all around while I stood blushing but Mr Shunt didn't mind at all and from then on Chiara called him Mr Shunt.

August 3 1991, we landed back in the Emergency Department where staff commented they hadn't seen Chiara for an unusually long time. They had become so accustomed to us presenting on a recurring basis for blocked shunts that they assumed she had been keeping well, until I told them she spent much of the previous nine months in Fielder's Ward, seriously ill.

Mr Hanieh was called to the Emergency Department without delay and he admitted her back into Fielders Ward. Continuing to vomit throughout the day and night, she spiked a temperature of 39.8 and again the microbiologists were put to work. Numerous blood tests were taken and another CAT scan revealed enlarged ventricles. The microbiologists solved the mystery when they discovered her spinal fluid was infected again with Meningitis, so Mr Hanieh removed the shunt for a temporary external one to enable the team to attack the infection. While carrying out the procedure, it appeared the blockage that initially caused the cysts, had cleared.

It was discussed that she may never need the shunt re-inserted into the cyst as it appeared to be draining on its own. I was cautious not to get over excited but at least she had a reprieve from one shunt, lessening the possibility of blockages, infections and all sorts of malfunctions. Two shunts doubled the risk of complications and only time would tell if she'd cope permanently without the second shunt. With the Meningitis brought under control we were able to leave the hospital and return to our lifestyle of living on the edge, continuing to play the waiting game.

Over the next three weeks, Chiara progressed well and took her first tentative steps for almost a year on Sunday September 1 1991. It happened to be both my Father's seventy-third birthday and Father's Day. We all cried. To see his youngest granddaughter try to walk to him was the best present my father had ever received, even though it was only three wobbly steps.

*Chiara wearing her eye patch is steadied by my mother before taking a few tentative steps towards my father*

Each day she practised using a walking frame on loan from the Physiotherapy Department. It made life much easier for both of us, as I no longer had to carry her everywhere or put her in a pram, which at four years of age, naturally she hated.

Tuesday September 3 1991, Chiara awoke vomiting and with Mr Hanieh away on holiday Professor Simpson was covering for him. Five minutes after our arrival at the hospital, even though she had improved, Professor Simpson admitted her into Fielders Ward for observation as a precaution. She remained well and we were discharged the following day. We picked up two of her young cousins and headed down to the beach; Chiara's favourite place and where I could relax.

Thursday was welcomed with more vomiting. We returned to hospital where Professor Simpson ordered a CAT scan that revealed another cyst had developed at the base of her brain. After lengthy discussions and a great deal of reassurance, we both agreed it was in Chiara's best interest to await Mr Hanieh's return. The following morning when Mr Hanieh returned she was relatively healthy so he sent us home.

Monday September 9 she had physiotherapy at the hospital and we called in to see Mr Hanieh. He asked Chiara to show him how well she could walk but she was more interested in helping Jan, his secretary, with the computer. Grudgingly she climbed off Jan's lap and walked a few unsteady paces for him. He then informed me he had booked another MRI scan to check the cysts but again, due to the waiting list at the Royal Adelaide Hospital, we were in for a lengthy wait.

I was determined to make it a fun time while we waited. We went to playgrounds that doubled as excellent physiotherapy sessions, the local lake, played games and had picnics in the park, or on the lounge room floor, depending on the weather.

On Friday September 13 Chiara underwent a two-hour assessment through the Queen Victoria Hospital's Long Term Follow-Up Unit. Considering she wasn't well and had undergone neurosurgery twenty-four times over the previous nine months, I didn't expect a great result, no-one did but she enjoyed doing the tasks.

The reason for conducting the test was to determine what she was capable of and what to expect after all she'd been through. A week later the results arrived in the mail and I was ecstatic to read she was above average in most things except gross motor skills which was understandable.

On Wednesday September 18 we attended Kindergarten (Kindy) for the first time. It was a huge achievement when previously any chance of a normal life was an impossible dream. Still unable to walk more than a few steps unaided, the Children's Services Department offered help on a Monday afternoon enabling me to leave Chiara with a Carer at Kindy, giving her some independence.

For the rest of the week I remained to help her manoeuvre around the Kindy grounds but I longed for more time out, just to sit and stare at a wall if I wanted to. I felt guilty even thinking it. The Children's Services Office promised extra help after Christmas but by then it would be too late and we wouldn't need it.

After restless nights, Chiara woke up screaming every morning. Exhausted, it was more than I could bear and more than she should have had to. I craved for her to stay well and pain free forever but it wasn't to be. Dribbling from the corner of her mouth while agitated and irritable, my sanity at breaking point, Chiara was in undeniable trouble.

Exhibiting those symptoms left no doubt the cyst was the problem and bypassing the Emergency Department, I took her straight to Mr Hanieh's office. An MRI scan booked, he allowed us to go back home to celebrate Dani's eighteenth birthday which was planned for that evening. We managed to enjoy the night celebrating without rushing back to hospital.

Attempting to maintain some semblance of social life with Chiara ill but stable, I joined a single parent's club and was delighted when we were invited along to a magnificent property for a barbecue in the countryside at Birdwood with all the other members. Chiara had a lovely time mixing with other children, while watching sheep and cattle grazing on the grassy hill nearby as vintage vehicles drove by, taking part in the annual Bay to Birdwood car rally.

Strolling around the impressive property, everyone took turns to help carry her. To see her sitting on a rock throwing pebbles into the creek against a magnificent hillside backdrop brought a tear to my eye as something so simple meant a great deal to me. Chiara hadn't seen sheep and cattle except in story books nor had she seen a creek or thrown pebbles into one.

On September 30, Dani's actual birthday, as per almost every special occasion, Chiara woke vomiting but thankfully settled quickly, so we didn't disturb Mr Hanieh. Steadily progressing physically and getting stronger, she wanted to be like other children, refusing to use the walking frame which resulted in constant falls but she was determined to walk again, unaided.

Tuesday October 8 1991 Chiara underwent the MRI scan. The next morning we sat in Mr Hanieh's office awaiting the results. When he appeared his eyes said it all. With that look of despair he lifted her into his arms, and as he took a deep breath, I heard the words I had been dreading.

'The cyst is now quite large and there's also two smaller ones; we must put the shunt back in.' It was the outcome I had expected but the disappointment was beyond measure. We can't go through it all again. We can't take much more. I was exhausted trying to be a good mother to Dani while constantly tending to her infirm sister, it was a dismal situation.

Mr Hanieh inserted the new shunt October 15. The previous operation on the cysts took six hours and therefore I expected that it would take as long, if not longer, with the thought of any more complications too horrendous to contemplate. Less than two hours later Mr Hanieh was standing next to me. I thought it was too soon for him to have finished. I thought I had lost her. Too frightened to ask how she was I stared into his eyes not sure I wanted to hear what he was about to say. 'We've finished.'

I nervously asked, 'How is she?' A man of very few words, he responded with a smile, 'Fine.'

'You've finished already?'

'Oh yes it was a relatively small procedure. We left a gap during the previous operation that allowed easy access.' With my heart pounding I thanked him and sat down an emotional mess. We had been expecting Chiara to go into the Intensive Care Unit after the surgery but she came out of the anaesthetic complaining of being hungry and demanding lunch. The following day she was happy and wanted to go home; the whole scenario I nervously expected didn't eventuate.

Saturday morning Mr Hanieh came to see Chiara and found her playing with a stethoscope in her ears doing her own 'observations.' He asked if she'd like to go home. She asked him to lift her out of bed and as he obliged she responded, 'Yes please.' Mr Hanieh cuddled her telling her she wasn't to get sick anymore. Her bandaged head resting on his shoulder, she found the strength to whisper, 'thank you, I'll come back and see you next week.'

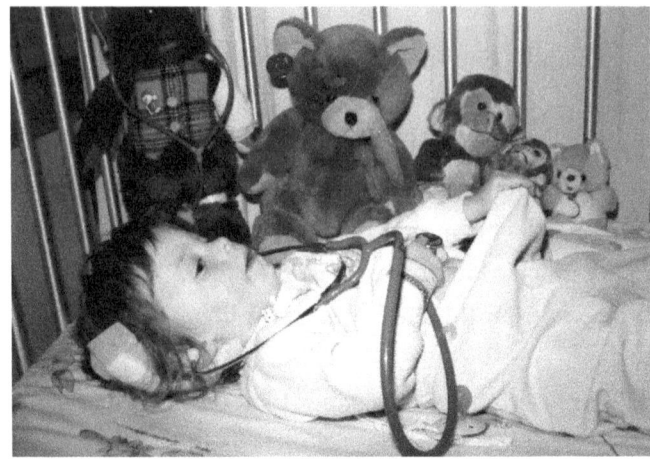
*Nurse Chiara*

No sooner had we arrived home the screaming started again. I was confident it was because the cysts had not fully drained and in time as they collapsed, she would be okay. On Monday October 21 we went back to Kindy where her Carer was waiting for her. I must confess I was relieved to see her so I could take a short break. Letting go of my hand in the doorway, Chiara precariously walked two steps unaided into her teacher's arms as tears streamed down my cheeks.

On the morning of December 1, I woke before Chiara, which was unusual. I had been trying to adapt to her early morning screaming episodes but that morning she was silent, sleeping peacefully beside me. Checking she was breathing I wasn't sure whether to be relieved or concerned when she opened her eyes and said, 'Hello mummy.'

'Hello darling are you okay?'

'I'm okay Mum. What can we do today? Mummy, are you alright, why are you crying?'

Elated I lifted her out of bed and up into the air. 'Oh Chiara you *are* okay. Those cysts have gone. I know they've gone because you aren't screaming at me anymore. How about we go to the beach today?'

'Yay, let's go to the beach. I'll go and find our bathers while you have your shower.'

My little girl was back. She was straining to speak but I was able to understand her better. The screaming had ceased, my sanity saved and I could even enjoy a long shower.

Friday December 10, Chiara underwent an MRI scan and for the first time I was confident of a good result telling Mr Hanieh I thought the cysts had collapsed. The next day I phoned him for the results. 'Well you are right again, Helen.'

*Chiara wearing her eye patch asks for chocolate*

# *Chiara starts school*

Chiara began her much anticipated first day at Saint Francis Xavier primary school Wynn Vale in July 1992. While she looked too small to be wearing a uniform and carrying a large bag, she was excited to be able to walk again and enjoy being a big school kid. I left the grounds with mixed feelings. Swollen with pride I was scared and anxious, worried she may take ill and no-one would notice.

I kept reassuring myself but I couldn't help worry. Chiara quickly made friends but before long we were back in hospital, and her newfound friends had moved on by the time she returned to school. It tormented me to discover she was spending most recess and lunchtimes sitting alone watching everyone else play. I wanted to go to the school every day just to play with her but it wasn't the answer.

I spent the days worrying about how lonely she was at the school she loved. When the situation didn't improve I spoke with her teachers and they organised a Buddy system to ensure someone would always be with her. She eventually found her best friend, Ali, and established a few other friendships too. She began to receive birthday party invitations. We had a touch of normality in our lives, if only for short stints, and I was also meeting new friends. I did some babysitting on a regular basis to help Chiara maintain friendships.

*First day of school*

Soon after befriending another first-grade classmate Emma, her mother discovered what Chiara had been through and approached me to say a friend of hers was offering to do a swim to raise funds on our behalf for the children's hospital. I was astounded but extremely thankful that someone we'd never met would be so generous to give up his time to help us raise money. The swim took place and a few more dollars found their way to the hospital with grateful thanks.

Word quickly spread amongst the school community and within weeks, a further five thousand dollars had been raised by the staff and families of St Francis Xavier School on behalf of Chiara. The next thing I knew, we were on television being interviewed about neurosurgery and shunts. At the end of the segment, the hospital switchboard unexpectedly went into meltdown, inundated with many viewers ringing to make donations.

My mother spent her retirement years as a China Painting teacher and many of her students and members of the China Painting fraternity recognised us on television, and they too wanted to help young neurosurgical patients at the children's hospital. An exhibition held at the Adelaide Convention Centre raised ten thousand dollars in one night which was presented to Mr Hanieh on our behalf. Although I continued to struggle financially, we were giving back by helping to raise awareness and in turn much needed dollars.

*Mr Hanieh receives $10,000 for the Neurosurgical Department.*

# *One shunt or two*

During November 1992 Chiara began experiencing excruciating pain in her head for no apparent reason. Mr Hanieh, confident it wasn't the shunt, referred us to a neurologist but when an Electroencephalogram (EEG) returned a negative result, we were sent back to Mr Hanieh who, still unconvinced it was shunt related, sent us back to neurology for another EEG which again returned a negative result. Again, back to see Mr Hanieh. Revolving doors had become part of our life.

Chiara was experiencing the onset of excruciating pain in her forehead, only to have it disappear within an hour or so, and resurface later in the day and again disappear. The neurologist ultimately ascertained the pain was caused by migraine headaches. Being from a family of migraine sufferers it was different to anything I had ever known about migraine behaviour. Chiara would have two or three episodes of pain a day for a number of days. The neurologist labelled them cluster migraines.

While my intuition was screaming cysts, I felt I couldn't question anyone because all tests returned negative results. Now Chiara had to tolerate intermittent insufferable headaches! The apparent migraines persisted for nine long, stressful and agonising months until August 1993 when Chiara rapidly deteriorated so I took her back to hospital.

For the first time in years Chiara and I were strangers to the staff in the Emergency Department. No-one on duty that day knew us. It came as a shock for me to realise all the Resident Medical Officers and registrars we had come to trust had moved on to other hospitals. Professor Simpson had retired, and we didn't recognise any of the nurses. We were back to square one and had to go over six years of medical history to the nurse at the desk and every doctor who came to assess Chiara. Mr Hanieh was overseas attending a convention. Apart from the trauma and stress, the biggest frustration having a chronically ill child is continuously repeating their extensive medical history.

The neurosurgery registrar arrived and I repeated Chiara's history all over again. He was a lovely man and I was confident in his ability but he didn't know us and he wasn't Mr Hanieh. He tried to reassure me a neurosurgeon from the Royal Adelaide Hospital was on standby if we needed him. It wasn't any consolation as I only trusted Mr Hanieh so it wouldn't matter how good any other surgeon was, the thought of someone else performing surgery on Chiara was inconceivable.

The registrar then left to refer to Chiara's five volumes of medical notes and to consult the neurosurgeon from the Royal Adelaide Hospital who ordered an MRI scan, the results of which revealed the cysts were building up again. I wasn't surprised. Chiara was admitted to Fielders Ward which was another jolt because the majority of the staff were new. We felt somewhat lost without familiar faces for support.

Later that day the registrar returned questioning how many shunts Chiara had. 'She has a ventricular peritoneal and a ventricular atrium shunt. The VP shunt is draining the fourth ventricle into the peritoneal cavity and the VA shunt is draining the cysts into her heart.'

'Helen are you absolutely certain there are two shunts, one of each?'

'Yes of course I'm sure. Why do you doubt me?'

'Because I can't find any mention anywhere in the notes of there being two shunts.'

'Doctor please, Chiara has had two shunts for nearly two years. Originally there were two joined into one that Mr Hanieh referred to as a 'piggy-back' VP shunt but with all her troubles in 1991 he gave her two independent ones. She definitely has two, a VP and a VA. The one in the cysts was removed temporarily but replaced, so for a short while she only had one but now she has two.'

'Helen we have a problem then because we can't find it in the notes anywhere that she has two so I'll have to re-consult the neurosurgeon from the RAH and tell him you are certain there are two shunts.'

'Doctor, I'd like to speak to him myself. What if he decides to operate? What is he going to operate on if he doesn't believe there's two?'

The registrar left and Chiara remained stable long enough to await Mr Hanieh's return. I had never been more relieved to see his face and he, in turn, was astonished to learn of the confusion relating to Chiara's *two* shunts. Surgery performed, *one* of the shunts revised, the cysts once again draining and the cluster migraines vanished after the surgery. Yet again, my earlier intuition proved to be right.

Dani remained my tower of strength throughout, sharing my anguish and anxiety while trying to maintain the appearance amongst her peers, of leading a conventional life. By this time at the age of twenty, she had gained full-time government employment on the other side of town, and with my blessing and understanding, moved out of home to be closer to her workplace. Chiara and I would have to manage without her phenomenal, much appreciated support.

\*\*\*

One morning while reading the paper, I learned the Labor Government had agreed to fund a second public Magnetic Resonance Imaging (MRI) scanner. The Women's and Children's Hospital put up a tremendous fight to have the new MRI installed there but the then Government, in their wisdom, ascertained it would be best situated at the Flinders Medical Centre even though, apparently at that time, the children's hospital had a much heavier neurosurgical caseload.

The decision not to install it at the children's hospital was outrageous in my opinion. Apart from saving children's lives, surely it would have generated monetary savings for the government. I wrote letters to newspapers and politicians in the hope someone would act. The Liberal State Minister of Health at that time agreed an MRI scanner located at the children's hospital would be more sensible and cost efficient. I didn't know how I was going to achieve it but I set out to try to rectify the situation.

I was determined the public, and in particular the South Australian Government, would be made aware of the plight our sickest, most vulnerable children faced. They not only deserved their own MRI scanner, it was their right to be afforded the best possible care. I wrote letters to anyone and everyone, I hounded politicians.

Chiara was six years old and with all the phone calls I was making she realised I was fighting for an MRI scanner for children. She shocked me when she asked if she could write her own letter to the Premier of South Australia to see if she could help.

One particular letter I wrote to a local newspaper editor resulted in my receiving a harsh phone call from an elected member of Parliament who had obviously looked up my home phone number in the telephone directory. I asked in my letter whether we had to wait for a politician to lose their own child before anything is done. He rang me to say he 'didn't appreciate the tone' of my letter.

I continued the fight, contacting a company in Sydney to obtain up-to-date information on the scanners, receiving word there was a new paediatric MRI one available, and the most exciting news was the children wouldn't need an anaesthetic. The new scanner was in excess of two million dollars so I became a bit of an activist to raise awareness of this new machine.

Money can't buy health but it can go a long way towards providing hospitals with essential equipment necessary to save lives, buying a patient some quality of life and a family, reassurance.

*Chiara's letter asking the Premier Lynn Arnold for an MRI scanner*

Someone was answerable to our children and their families. The deplorable situation had to be rectified. Australian children should not be going without proper medical care and attention especially when it appeared to me that the government had the money to buy them an MRI scanner.

# *A special Christmas service*

In December 1993 a small band of dedicated staff members from the Women's and Children's Hospital recognised the need to do more to support families of sick children. They took it upon themselves to do something truly amazing. A special Christmas service was organised in the Cathedral across the road from the hospital for children with life threatening illnesses and their families. They also included the families of children who had sadly lost their battle for life.

On the morning of the service a lump started forming in the back of Chiara's neck that quickly grew to the size of a chicken's egg. Mr Hanieh assured me it was nothing to worry about and sent us home. That evening I took her to the Cathedral.

When we arrived it was apparent she was too ill to participate so the organisers suggested I join the procession and carry her. I happily agreed. All of the children carried a bunch of helium balloons down the aisle and we joined them. A choir of angelic voices sang Christmas hymns as we all slowly made our way towards the altar.

It was a poignant sight as ribbons and balloons swayed high in the air. The children placed their balloons at the altar and the priest began the service. Everyone was then handed candles to light and place at the foot of the altar in remembrance of children who had passed and to honour those gallantly striving to survive.

Families and friends wrote the names of special children on stars and placed them on an enormous Christmas tree. We then each took a balloon outside into the church grounds and simultaneously let them go. In an instant, brightly coloured balloons filled the skies bringing to an end a highly emotional service with most of the congregation teary-eyed.

As the evening progressed Chiara continued to worsen and I stressed over whether to take her home from the Cathedral or back to hospital. Remembering Mr Hanieh said she was okay, I opted to go home. Once tucked up in bed she said Jason was in her room again. She hadn't mentioned him for two years and was adamant he was back. 'He *really* is here Mummy; he's sitting in my rocking chair. He's my friend and he's come back to look after me.'

Early the next day she hadn't improved, so I dressed her and laid her on the couch to watch television while I went to get organised for a return to hospital. When I walked back into the room I sat her on my lap, and noticed the lump was oozing a substance resembling thick creamy coloured glue. Trying not to panic I picked up the telephone, bypassed the hospital Emergency Department and rang Mr Hanieh direct. 'Helen come straight in and I will meet you in Emergency.'

With my heart pounding, I drove too fast and collected a speeding fine along the way. Mr Hanieh greeted me with words I had never heard him say before, 'Helen this could be very serious but we won't know until we get the results from the swabs.' I was shocked but not surprised. With a drip inserted, the microbiologists once again worked to combat Chiara's infection. I sat crying, wishing it wasn't happening, wanting it to all go away.

Chiara was extremely lucky as the infection was deemed superficial and quickly brought under control leaving Mr Hanieh, Chiara and I immensely relieved. With his young daughter Emma at his side, he told Chiara she could go home but Chiara wouldn't leave until I took a photo of her with Emma. Regardless of how sick Chiara was, her little face always lit up whenever Emma came to visit with her father. We returned home a few days later able to look forward to spending Christmas at home.

*Chiara with Emma Hanieh*

## *Wishes come true*

Early in 1994 the Make a Wish Foundation recognised Chiara's courageous battle for survival. Elizabeth from the Foundation contacted me for details regarding Chiara's health and within days official 'Wish' forms arrived in the letterbox. Even though Chiara was chronically ill without a cure or prognosis, I didn't think she'd qualify for a 'wish' as I thought it was only for terminally ill children. I opted to return the completed forms anyway.

We visited our General Practitioner (GP) to get treatment for an ear infection Chiara had developed. While examining her he casually mentioned returning his forms to Make a Wish. I remembered being asked for the names of doctors so the Foundation could contact them for verification. The GP said Chiara deserved the granting of a wish. Thanking him, we left with a prescription for her ear infection and the encouragement for once, something fantastic might happen for our little wounded soldier.

I refrained from mentioning the Make a Wish Foundation to Chiara for fear of arousing her hopes, so she was confused. 'Mummy what were you and the doctor talking about?' Playing down the conversation I said it was nothing she should be concerned about. The following month we went to Chiara's paediatrician for a routine check-up where he too mentioned he had returned the Make a Wish forms. He said Chiara deserved to have a wish granted.

As we were at the hospital anyway, I took her to visit Mr Hanieh who was always happy to see her healthy. Mr Hanieh obviously loved his special patient and the relationship between them will always be treasured. Entering his office, I heard, 'Hello Chiara.' It was unmistakably his voice but where was he? As we neared the desk, he appeared from around the corner where he had been faxing his forms back to Make a Wish.

Mr Hanieh led us into his office where he sat behind his desk. Chiara climbed up on his lap and gently stroked his face. He said it was great news to have her nominated and that he was more than happy to sign the forms. I was amazed at all the support we received from a remarkable group of doctors.

As the days turned into weeks the thought of any wish becoming reality was beginning to fade until Elizabeth rang to say they wanted to come out to meet us and ask Chiara what her biggest wish was. It was difficult to keep my excitement under control. Nothing like this had ever happened to us. I started trembling as tears of joy ran down my face. Arrangements were made for the visit to take place the following Saturday. Elizabeth and Nicola were two of a number of exceptional people who gave freely of their time to the Foundation and delighted in seeing the reaction of 'wish' families.

The following Saturday, Elizabeth and Nicola arrived. After greetings and introductions were taken care of it was time to discuss formalities. 'Chiara if you could have anything in the whole wide world, or go anywhere you want to go what, or where would it be?'

Without hesitation Chiara replied, 'I want to go on an aeroplane to Movieworld. I want to see Tweety.'

'Well Chiara, we are here to try to make your wish come true.' Elizabeth then turned to me and said, 'Chiara's wish will have to go before the Board so it may take a month or so, but I really don't think there'll be any problems.'

'We'll look forward to hearing from you. I cannot possibly thank you enough for coming and trying to make this happen. It's very exciting for us. Thank you again.'

As we waved goodbye our excitement was electrifying. Chiara was beginning to grasp there was a possibility we might all be going on the holiday of a lifetime where she would get to meet Tweety Bird.

Approximately six weeks later the phone rang. 'Hi Helen, it's Elizabeth from Make a Wish. I'm ringing to inform you the Board has considered Chiara's wish and have made a decision. You, Dani and Chiara are all off to the Gold Coast for a week and you will be provided with spending money so you won't have to worry.'

Choking back tears, my voice crackling I managed to respond, 'Oh Elizabeth I don't believe it. I'm completely shocked at the generosity. We've never had a real holiday before. I don't know what to say but thank you.'

'I have some details for you and all we need to know is when you'd like to go. You can leave on Saturday if you like for a mid-year Christmas in the mountains or you can go whenever you want to.'

'This weekend? Oh no it's too soon, I have too much to organise and I don't even own a suitcase.'

'That's fine you decide a date and get back to me whenever you're ready. I'll wait to hear from you.'

'Thank you Elizabeth I can't believe it, it doesn't seem real. I need time to take it all in so please don't give me any details now, I can't think straight and I'll only forget. I'll ring you back in a day or so when my head stops spinning.'

I hung up the phone and caught my breath. It was the most fantastic news we had ever received. We were going on a *real* holiday. Chiara's dream would come true and I couldn't wait to get to school to tell her the news.

'Guess what Chiara, guess what.'

'I don't know mummy, what.'

'Do you remember meeting Elizabeth and Nicola when they came to our house and asked you what your biggest wish was?'

'Yes I remember.'

'Well, Elizabeth rang me today to say your wish is going to come true. You, Dani and I are going to see Tweety Bird. We're going to fly in a big plane to Queensland.'

Chiara was so excited she started twirling around falling down in front of me as school children looked on. 'Yahoo! Yippee! We're going to see Tweety, we're going to see Tweety,' she kept squealing.

I helped her to her feet and had never seen her so deliriously happy. For once in her life we could forget surgeries, anaesthetics, drips, drains, butterfly needles and blood tests, CAT scans, X-rays, MRI's, doctors, nurses and pain. We were going to transcend the nightmare existence for seven fun-filled days. We would leave on 9 July and return 16 July. The timing couldn't have been better.

The shunt *wasn't* going to claim Chiara's seventh birthday because we would spend it enjoying the thrill of the Gold Coast, not in the confines of a hospital ward. During conversations with Elizabeth and Nicola I mentioned Humphrey Bear brought Chiara out of a comatose state in 1991. When we arrived at the airport there to meet us was none other than Humphrey Bear who had come to farewell his special little friend on the trip of a lifetime. (Humphrey's full name is actually Humphrey Bear Bear).

Being witness to that moment in departure lounge number ten at the Adelaide Airport was pure magic. Chiara pleaded with Humphrey to join us but he didn't think to pack a suitcase and the plane was geared up ready for take-off. Chiara and Humphrey bid their farewells on the steps of the 737. We were privileged to fly first-class with the now defunct Ansett Airlines. We had a lovely pilot who invited us to check out the cockpit while allowing Chiara to wear his hat.

Robyn, another Foundation member, was there to greet us at Coolangatta Airport. We were chauffeured to our luxurious twenty-fourth floor apartment towering high above Cavill Mall in Surfers

Paradise. I could easily have spent the entire week just lapping up the luxury in the magnificent apartment.

*Chiara and Humphrey B Bear*

The week ahead was all organised on our behalf, however should we so desire to squeeze anything else in, it was available for the asking. The stunning views from the apartment overlooking the rolling seas to our right and the magnificent Nerang River meandering to our left were breath-taking. Waking to such a glorious view every morning, basking on the balcony while enjoying a hearty breakfast, was definitely my idea of the ultimate in a luxurious lifestyle.

Seven days wasn't going to be long enough to recharge my well-worn batteries and fully appreciate all Queensland's exhilarating playground had to offer. I was already pondering how to make another extended visit happen.

Enjoying our first hours on the sunny Gold Coast we merrily played the role of tourists, wandering up and down Cavill Mall, in and out of all the unique shops. We had a sensational time wandering around and sight-seeing. Pacific Fair was by far the best shopping experience we had ever enjoyed and I imagined how fantastic it would be to recreate such a complex on the banks of our River Torrens in Adelaide.

Early in the morning on Monday 11 July Dani and I were singing Happy Birthday watching Chiara meticulously open each present. Never one to rush things, we waited patiently as she carefully pulled back each piece of sticky tape, so as not to tear any of the paper. Dani, not possessing the patience of her sister, wanted to rip open the presents. 'Chiara wouldn't you like some help?' she asked but Chiara wouldn't allow it. 'No thank you Dani, I can manage.'

Our Con-X-ions mini bus arrived at 9am to take us to Dreamworld. Once we were settled on board, Richard the bus driver announced to a captive audience that a very special young lady was celebrating her all-important seventh birthday. He had the entire busload of people singing Happy Birthday to a rather shy and slightly overwhelmed Chiara. It was a lovely surprise and testament to the carefree people in Paradise. I was to learn Richard had been hand-picked to drive us that morning.

Arriving at Dreamworld we were warmly welcomed in the Very Important Person room and advised to be at the Plaza Restaurant by twelve midday. Chiara, not afraid of anything, was keen to ride on everything that moved. Her only problem was that she wasn't tall enough to go on many of the rides. Dani, who didn't share the thrill seeking enthusiasm of her brave sister, was more content to remain on the sidelines armed with the camera. I was wrong thinking that Dani would accompany Chiara on the rides, while I'd be the one happily gathering the memories.

At midday we arrived at the Plaza Restaurant as instructed, to meet the representative from Guest Relations, the cuddly Kenny and Belinda Koala, as well as Dreamworld's resident musicians playing their unique brand of music especially for us on their drums. A surprise birthday party had been organised by the staff and they even made a Koala shaped cake bearing the message 'Happy Birthday Chiara.'

Wishes come true 157

*Chiara's Surprise Birthday at Dreamworld*

That day we were given many memories to carry for the rest of our lives. At 5pm Richard returned as promised. Exhilarated but exhausted, we boarded the mini-bus for our return trip.

Before heading up to the apartment we dropped our film in to be developed into the laboratory situated in the same complex, and then went to our favourite café on the beachfront. Dani and I enjoyed large thick pieces of whiting, complete with the most delicious salad we had ever eaten. Chiara ordered half a chicken and salad and to our surprise did an excellent job devouring it. We had never seen her eat so much and when she finished we strolled back to collect our photos. 'A film for Barr please.'

'Oh,' was all the shop assistant said. What was that look for I wondered as she walked across to the supervisor. Looking up the supervisor asked, 'Was that for Barr?'

'Yes. Is there a problem?'

'I'm really sorry Mrs Barr, yes there is a problem. Your film was blank. I'm sorry to have to tell you this it's the worst part of the job, telling people their film was blank.'

I held back the tears. 'It can't be blank, not *this* film. It's the film of my daughter's birthday today and we're here compliments of Make a Wish. The people at Dreamworld gave my daughter a surprise birthday party and it's all on that film. I can never get those moments back, they're gone forever. We can *never* repeat today. Our holiday means so much to us and to many people back home and now we don't have the photos to show them. How could I have been so stupid? It doesn't make any sense. What could possibly have gone wrong?'

While I babbled and poured my heart out, the sales assistant stood, holding the blank film, looking as though she was about to burst into tears herself. I felt stupid, she didn't need my problems.

'I have no idea why it's happened but it's usually one of two things,' she said.

'What two things? What could I have done?' I couldn't wait for her to get the words out perhaps there was a simple explanation.

'We sometimes find it's because the film hasn't been inserted properly and doesn't wind on, even though you think it has, or it's a blank film.'

'What do you mean a blank film?'

'Could you have given us a new unused film instead of the right one?'

'Oh no, it's not possible. I wouldn't have done that. I wish it were that simple. No those photos are gone forever, never to be replaced.'

Dejected we returned to our apartment. Once inside I placed the camera, my bag and keys on the breakfast bar. I saw another film there, the last of the films I'd brought from Adelaide. Could it have been a faulty one? Could the film on the breakfast bar be the one with

Dreamworld on it? No, that's not possible. I wasn't about to take a chance on that film being a reject too, I decided to throw it out.

Picking it up to put in the bin something was driving at me to take it to the developers. That film hasn't anything on it, it's a new one, I thought. Too tired and depressed to fight the strange force, I had nothing to lose by putting the film in, after all it was only going in the bin anyway. I told the girls I'd return in a few minutes, locked the door and quickly ran downstairs.

Handing over the film, I apologised to the salesperson for wasting their time but I needed them to develop it as I had a very strange feeling driving me to do so. Imagine the jubilation when the salesperson approached the counter saying, 'Here you go Mrs Barr, your photos.'

I raced back up to the twenty-fourth floor apartment, collapsed in a heap on the couch to reflect and enjoy the photos. I have no idea how the film on the breakfast bar contained the photos, considering I took the film from Dreamworld out of the camera at the shop and handed it to the salesperson before we headed back to the apartment. It shall forever remain a mystery.

On Tuesday morning we shopped once again. I loved how cheap much of the clothing, food and souvenirs were compared to the prices in South Australia. It added to the fun and enjoyment being able to afford some bargains. That afternoon we were in a boat on the tranquil Nerang River courtesy of Shangri-La Cruises. It was a perfect way to spend a lazy Tuesday afternoon and Chiara was so exhausted she fell asleep.

We went to movie world on Wednesday morning, where once again we were met by Guest Relations in their Very Important Persons room and handed a timetable and instructions of what to see and do. Chiara loved all the Looney Tune characters and was ecstatic to find her much adored Tweety Bird. While we were standing watching a show featuring all the characters including Tweety, I turned to give Dani some money to buy a drink.

In those few seconds, with my back turned, Chiara was trying to climb up on to the stage. Given the nod from the compere I lifted her up and for a short time she was part of the show.

Dani insisted we go into the arena to watch the Police Academy Cops show and it was the first time we'd laughed so much in a long time. The studio tour was worth the wait in the queue. It was another memorable day.

On Thursday we ventured to the Currumbin Bird Sanctuary and although fatigued, Chiara refused to sit in a stroller, so Dani and I took turns to carry her.

*Chiara enjoying Currumbin Bird Sanctuary*

At the end of the day we dropped our film off for developing then went to get some dinner. Back in the apartment we found our bathers and made our way down to the sixth floor for a spa. I couldn't get over how well Chiara was doing. Dani and I were both nursing sore aching feet but Chiara wasn't complaining.

Friday we were at Seaworld and met as usual by Guest Relations giving us maps and timetables for shows not to be missed. Before I knew it we were ushered into a helicopter. There wasn't time for a 'Thank you but no thank you.' I hate flying at the best of times and the thought of a helicopter ride scared me but with Dani flatly refusing to get on board and Chiara already strapped into her seat, I had no alternative. We were up and away.

Next it was onto the Dolphin show where we were treated to a behind-the-scenes adventure and introduced to the dolphins, even getting the opportunity to pat them.

*Meeting the Dolphins*

*A very tired Chiara agrees to let Helen put her in the little dolphin stroller*

An over-tired Chiara gave in, permitting us to put her in one of the cute dolphin strollers available for use at Sea World. She enjoyed the rest of the day being wheeled around, and would jump out every time we approached any rides.

Our perfect dream holiday was nearing an end and I lost count of how many rolls of film we had used. I congratulated myself on developing them each day instead of waiting until we arrived home. Friday night was a time for packing and I was determined we'd go out in style.

Across the road from our apartment, stood the Bavarian Steak House. I'd been mesmerised each night standing on our balcony watching it's flashing fairy lights beckoning us to indulge. On our final night I succumbed and telephoned to make a booking. A cheery voice answered and introduced herself as Di. We arrived shortly after and promptly escorted to our table. When we had all decided on what to eat, I went to the counter to place our order with money in hand. I was told, 'Put your money away, your meals are our pleasure.' Moments later Di arrived to welcome us. 'Hello Helen, my name is Di, I took your booking on the phone. If there is anything at all you need, please don't hesitate to ask. I'm going to move you to another table, follow me.' Single file we obediently marched behind Di. We'd been moved to the best seats in the house, directly in front of the floorshow. 'There you go that's much better,' she said.

'Thank you Di. I'd like to introduce my daughters. My eldest Dani, and this is Chiara whose wishes are all coming true. Thank you for your kindness.'

'Helen, it's nothing. It's the least I can do. I want you all to have a lovely night and enjoy yourselves. I'll check on you later.' The floorshow began comprising three musicians dressed in traditional Bavarian costume. Chiara was invited onto the stage to play the bells alongside other children and she was absolutely enchanted, concentrating on the task she was given. Boris the Bavarian appeared and made a big fuss of her. We were spoilt by Di and the team at the Steak House. It was a perfect way to wind up our week away, relaxed and happy.

As we were about to leave we noticed a gift shop and stood admiring the souvenirs when Di appeared. 'Chiara what would you like?' An ecstatic Chiara was handed an exquisite tiny Bavarian chalet and a small replica of the bell she'd played on stage. Di then turned her attention to Dani and asked what she would like. Di couldn't do enough for us. She was such a warm-hearted person, an individual capable of restoring one's faith in humanity.

We were treated like royalty from the moment we left Adelaide. The people of the Gold Coast knew how to look after their tourists. Make a Wish and Queenslanders took a sick child and her family into their hearts and made an impossible dream come true. We have cherished memories from that week away which saw Chiara the healthiest she'd ever been. It was nice to hear my girls laugh during that holiday. We felt as though we were a normal family doing what so many other families take for granted.

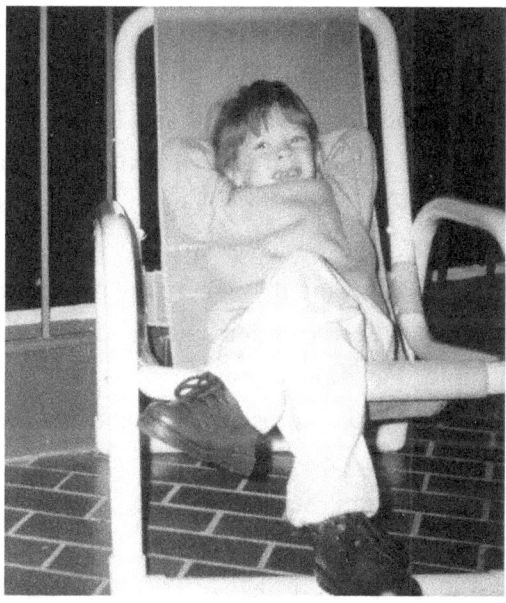

*Chiara relaxes in Queensland*

## *History repeats itself*

August 7 1994 Chiara was behaving atrociously while I was trying to get her ready for school. It was only 9am and I was already exhausted. At 3.15 pm I returned to pick her up, relieved to see her smiling face. The following morning was a carbon copy of the day before with her behaviour again intolerable.

Fighting the obvious I wanted to ignore the pattern that was all too familiar. The day progressed uninterrupted and again at home time, I found her happy. Watching television that afternoon she calmly mentioned a headache. My stomach churned but I chose to ignore it, suggesting she move back away from the television. The headache wasn't mentioned again and she slept soundly all night.

With the headache forgotten the next morning she went off to school. Sonya, a close friend, called in for a morning coffee. Those were the days I enjoyed the most, carefree, with nothing better to do than enjoy the simplicity of a coffee and chat with a girlfriend. My time-out, come-what-may days.

As Sonya was leaving, a car pulled up in the driveway. It was Gary. I didn't expect him to ever darken my doorstep again but I did want him to acknowledge Chiara, and be a father to his daughter. Before I had time to question his presence he shamelessly asked me to marry him. After all he put us through did he really think I would actually marry him?

I didn't have any idea where he was at in his life, what he'd been doing or where he was living but I remember sarcastically thinking his wife must've kicked him out, so he was back to try his luck with me. I was beyond caring and came to realise long ago that he obviously thought I was a convenient option for him. If he was genuine, surely he would have tried to slowly rebuild a relationship, not arrive unannounced and expect me to welcome him with open arms, wipe away all the grief and accept a marriage proposal. I didn't want him back and after telling him I would never re-enter into a relationship or marry him, he looked at me momentarily, turned and left.

Later I went to collect Chiara from school. As I walked into the grounds her teacher anxiously greeted me. 'Helen, Chiara isn't well. We went for a walk and she was fine holding my hand but without warning she collapsed. It only happened a few minutes ago. I didn't ring you because I knew you'd be on your way to pick her up.'

'Oh no Julie where is she?'

'She's in the classroom.'

Chiara was non-responsive and pale. Her eyes were glazed and unable to focus. I lifted her into my arms and with no time to call an ambulance, I placed her in the car. I had taken the advice of a friend some months before and replaced my pager with a mobile phone. Blessing modern technology I phoned the hospital from the car to inform them we were on our way. I drove wondering how I ever managed without a mobile phone.

When we reached the Emergency Department I was grateful to see familiar faces who took one look at Chiara and didn't hesitate to page the neurosurgical registrar, who in turn urgently contacted Mr Hanieh. Chiara hadn't been in hospital since Christmas 1993, it was now August 1994.

After assessing her, even though she had started to improve, Mr Hanieh turned to me, 'Helen it's time to check what's going on again.

I'll order an MRI and hopefully she'll get in early next week. Until then, there's not a lot more we can do. I know you can look after her at home, so go, and I'll ring you with the details of the MRI appointment. If she gets any worse come straight back.' My frustration at not having an MRI scanner at the children's hospital returned, although it was comforting to know Mr Hanieh was happy with my capability to look after Chiara at home.

'Well Chiara, you look a bit better now, so mum can take you home until I can get you in for a scan.' Sitting on my lap she put her hand out for him to hold as I thanked him for coming in. He asked how we enjoyed our holiday.

'Oh we had the best holiday. It was really hard to come back to reality. I didn't expect to be here so soon though because while we were away Chiara was the best she's ever been. It was like having a healthy seven-year-old and a normal life for a whole week. She had a fantastic time. I think we need to go back.'

'That's great that you all had a good time you deserve it. I saw your 'thank you' letter to Make a Wish and the people of Queensland in the Sunday Mail newspaper, it was excellent.'

'It was the only way I could think of to thank everyone who made it possible for us. Make a Wish can sure do with the publicity. Hopefully it will help to raise some money for them because they do a phenomenal job.' Apparently it's not uncommon for seriously ill children to stay well while on their special Make a Wish holiday.

Driving home Chiara started feeling better and ate a packet of Twisties while asking to play with friends. We were back re-living the time-bomb existence and all I could do was try to prepare psychologically to face the next inevitable round, at any given second. We settled down to enjoy an uneventful evening and early night.

Back at school the next morning I swung into my get-set mode; paying bills, putting petrol in the car, doing the housework and ensuring the washing was all done and hung out to dry, not left in the machine. We were back to a second-by-second existence knowing any

## History repeats itself 167

second could spell disaster. There's nothing worse than Chiara taking ill at a time when there isn't any petrol in the car, no money in the purse and bills unpaid.

Two days later Mr Hanieh rang with the MRI appointment details. 'Helen we've done the best we can but we can't get her into the Royal Adelaide MRI scanner for two weeks.'

'Two weeks! What if she gets worse in the meantime?'

'We'll if she does, we'll have to operate without the benefit of the MRI results. There won't be any more time to wait.' Saying goodbye, I put the receiver down angry we had to wait two weeks.

When the day of her appointment finally arrived, the MRI receptionist handed me a questionnaire aimed at improving anything and everything regarding their MRI unit. I laughed as I took it in my hand thinking, 'Fancy giving *me* one of these.' I knew it wasn't the fault of the staff that the children had to wait, I was just angry at the government for not supplying the children with their own MRI unit.

The staff were all wonderful and I could not have asked for better treatment for Chiara whenever she was in their care. I lifted her up onto the sliding bed, carefully placing her head into what we called the helmet. The scanner sounds like a jackhammer so she wore a set of headphones with music playing to help drown out the noise.

Unable to reach her hand, I stood holding her foot as she lay bravely undergoing the scan. Forty-five minutes later the jack hammering ceased and she'd fallen asleep, probably due to the constant pounding sound. The results revealed a functioning shunt. Chiara had suffered yet another intermittent blockage so a few days later she returned to school while I played the waiting game, not knowing when the next blockage would occur.

A week later I received word our Commonwealth and State Governments were combining to fund a brand new state-of-the-art MRI scanner at a cost of $2.2 million to replace the seven-year-old MRI at the Royal Adelaide Hospital. I telephoned the Health Commission, politicians and the hospital but no-one could tell me why the new scanner wasn't going to the children's hospital. All I could ascertain was the old one would apparently become spare parts. Meanwhile the children still had to wait.

September 1994 the Women's and Children's Hospital caught me by surprise when they presented me with a Certificate of Appreciation for my participation on a few of their committees, helping to oversee the amalgamation process and striving to make improvements. As a long term consumer I raised awareness and funds while making administration and politicians aware of that which hadn't been evident to them. I accepted their acknowledgement on behalf of the children, their parents and families, and everyone else who had helped me.

On Wednesday September 14, 1994 I was at my neighbour's house consoling her on the sudden loss of her partner who had been killed in a tragic accident. At 3pm as I was about to leave to collect Chiara from school my mobile phone rang. 'Hello Helen, Chiara isn't well again. She's in the sick room and she looks terrible.'

'I'm on my way. Please comfort her. I'll be there in five minutes.'

'I'm so sorry Jo. I have to leave, but I'll get back to you when I can. We may have to go to hospital. Chiara's shunt has been playing up so it's probably blocked again.' I arrived at the school to find her an awful colour and holding her head in agony, she wasn't responding. I called an ambulance and left the car at the school so I could travel with her. I organised my brother Greg to pick my car up. As we neared the Emergency entrance Chiara began to respond.

Mr Hanieh arrived soon after us and said she needed an urgent MRI. He would ensure she gets in the next day, so for the first time we only had to wait twenty-four hours. It was almost as good as having an MRI scanner on site at the children's hospital. The result was negative so we were sent home. Three days later Chiara was again in severe pain. I asked her to show me where it hurt. 'Down here behind my ear.' she replied. I gently ran a finger along the shunt tube but unable to feel anything, told her to hop into bed and the pain would go away.

'Ouch Mummy it really hurts. I need Mr Hanieh to stop this pain.'

'Let me have another feel then. Oh now I can feel a lump, lie down for a while and see if you feel better while I ring him.'

I walked from the bedroom to the kitchen and straight back to discover her writhing in pain. 'Mummy the pain really hurts. I can't stand it.' The lump had suddenly grown to about the size of a large marble. I was extremely worried as it began to resemble the infected lump she had during Christmas in 1993.

With an infection ruled out, Mr Hanieh ordered a CAT scan, which revealed the shunt had come apart from the chamber behind her ear, causing a very painful build-up of fluid, resulting in her undergoing her fortieth operation to reconnect the shunt.

Throughout her life of pain and surgeries Chiara rarely ever cried but the next day she was crying and screaming in agony. Painkillers were administered intravenously but as the hours dragged by the pain increased, so another CAT scan was booked in the hope of revealing the cause. The result showed a working shunt and without an explanation for the pain, Chiara was discharged.

# PART THREE

# *Mary MacKillop*

It was October 1994 and with Chiara suffering unrelenting pain we were back to revolving doors between Mr Hanieh and the neurologist while they both tried in vain to determine the cause. With a heavy heart, a bewildered Mr Hanieh said there wasn't anything more they could do and we would have to wait and see what manifested. After all the years, all the heartbreak and forty operations we needed another miracle to relieve Chiara's uncompromising brutal pain.

Sleep deprived, I was at breaking point with Chiara too frail to walk, she was barely tolerating the pain, and her behaviour was atrocious. She was very ill and we had no idea what was wrong, leaving me heartbroken and helpless, not knowing what to do and how to help her other than to spend my days holding and comforting her.

In January 1995, one week before the beatification of Mary MacKillop, the pain and difficult behaviour continued. Without the strength to walk, Chiara had to be carried most of the time and she couldn't be bothered talking. I was exhausted and decided to take her to visit my parents in the hope it would take her mind off the pain. While I was driving she told me about a dream she had the night before. It was the first time in days that she was actually talking.

'Mummy I had a really strange dream last night.'

'Did you darling? Why was it strange?'

'Because I dreamt about Mary MacKillop.'

'What?' I almost drove off the road. Even though Dani was attending Mary MacKillop College when Chiara was born, she had been too ill all her life to have known anything about Mary McKillop or, even the name of Dani's school. I couldn't understand how Chiara could have dreamt about her.

As casually as possible I asked, 'What do *you* know about Mary MacKillop?'

'Nothing, I just dreamt about her.'

I expected the conversation to end there as she was struggling to talk but I continued in the hope of hearing more about her dream.

'Well if you don't know anything about her then how do you know it was Mary MacKillop in your dream?'

'Because she told me that's what her name was.'

Absolutely gobsmacked, I asked, 'Well if you dreamt about her what did she look like?'

'She looked like Mary.'

'Mary who?' I asked. 'Oh mum you know Mary.'

'Oh *that* Mary. Yes of course, Jesus' mother Mary. Is that who you dreamt about?'

'No mum, not *that* Mary. I told you, she said her name was Mary MacKillop.'

I was intrigued. 'Do you remember anything else, or what she was wearing?'

'Well, I could only see her face.'

'What do you mean you could only see her face?'

'Because she was wearing this thing around her head that went around her face like this.'

Chiara gestured a hand movement circling her own face around her forehead and down around her chin. Then she repeated, 'She was wearing this thing around her face and it went down her back like this.' As she spoke she moved her hand down from her head over her shoulder and down her back. I recognised her description and hand movements as trying to describe a nun's habit and veil but she could never have seen one, or a nun for that matter.

I asked Chiara if Mary had said anything else in the dream. 'She just kept saying to me over and over, come to me Chiara, come but I don't know what she meant.'

In disbelief I asked if she remembered anything else. 'Well only that she was standing in a little old schoolhouse and she had her arms out to me like this and kept saying, Come to me Chiara, come to me.' A shiver ran down my spine. To my knowledge, Schoolhouse and Mary MacKillop were words Chiara would never have heard.

By the time we arrived at my parents' house, my head was reeling. I parked under the carport and asked Chiara to wait in the car for a minute. I ran inside and asked my parents if either of them had ever mentioned Mary MacKillop to Chiara. Puzzled they asked, 'What ever are you talking about?'

'Chiara just told me she had a strange dream last night and I need to know whether either of you have ever mentioned anything about her.' In unison they replied, 'No never.' I collected Chiara from the car and asked her to tell my parents about her dream. Word for word she told them exactly what she had told me.

After hearing about her dream my mother said, 'This is incredible. What you *don't* know is that we've been praying to Mary MacKillop and so too have other members of the family and some of our friends. We've all been praying for a miracle but we've never told Chiara.'

The day after Chiara's dream, I had a strange urge to take her to Sydney for the beatification of Mary MacKillop which was due to take place on January 19 1995. I deliberated on whether the 'Come to me Chiara' meant I was about to lose her and it made me feel anxious and unsettled. None of it made any sense but I began praying to Mary, if for no other reason than because others were, and to plead with her to stop the pain and tone down Chiara's sometimes out of control behaviour.

That night, restless and unable to sleep, I tried to devise how we could afford to make the trip. The next day I resolved to accept it wasn't possible due to our dire financial position and time-bomb existence. I put all thoughts of travelling to the beatification out of my head.

Three days after Chiara's dream, her father arrived on our doorstep to give us a cheque for $2000. I hadn't seen or spoken to him since his marriage proposal and he didn't know anything of my aspiration to take Chiara to Sydney. He had apparently cashed in an insurance policy and told me to use the money however I wanted. I briefly explained Chiara's dream to him and expected him to think I had lost my mind. I asked if I could use the money to take Chiara to Sydney and he replied, 'Use it for anything you want. I'm really sorry for everything I've put you all through.'

His words were empty and meaningless but his cheque was greatly appreciated. Everything was falling into place. I worried he might have thought he could buy his way back into our lives. If that was the case, he was sadly mistaken. I wanted the satisfaction of throwing the cheque back at him but it was the exact amount I needed to get Chiara to Sydney so I thanked him and sent him on his way.

I phoned Sister Margaret, a nun at Mary MacKillop College in Kensington, to discuss Chiara's dream, and I asked if there was a pilgrimage to Sydney planned. She told me there was but it was completely booked out, including the accommodation. She was very excited to hear about the dream and I was astounded when she said Chiara could possibly be Mary MacKillop's second miracle, which would pave the way for her sainthood. I was disappointed there wasn't room for us on the pilgrimage. I didn't have the confidence to take Chiara on my own, while she was so ill and too weak to walk more than a few steps at a time.

Reassessing my thoughts, I reasoned it would be too great a risk to take her so far away from Mr Hanieh. What would I do if she took ill? Then I pondered if the 'Come to me' in Chiara's dream meant for her to go to Sydney, and if so then she would surely be okay, at least for a few days. Not knowing Sydney or where we would need to be, and having to organise flights and accommodation was too daunting for me to contemplate. We wouldn't be going to the beatification and

I would never know what Chiara's dream really meant and why she would have even dreamt about Mary MacKillop.

Two hours later Sister Margaret rang me back to say everything was arranged for us and all we had to do was arrive at the airport. I was stunned. I worried how Chiara would manage a plane flight but decided if it was what we were meant to do, then she would cope with the pain, and I would cope with her behaviour and having to carry her most of the time. We were going to Sydney!

# *The Beatification*

A woman named Joy thankfully had agreed to meet us at the airport to accompany us on our journey. I studied every person for someone matching her description and wondered why Chiara kept looking around and seemed upset. I asked her what was wrong. 'Mummy, he's not here. Where is he? He *has* to come.'

'Chiara, what are you talking about? Who isn't here?'

'Humphrey. He came to see me off when we went to Queensland. Why isn't he here now?' I tried to explain Humphrey's absence but it didn't help. It hadn't occurred to me she would expect him to be at the airport.

We eventually found Joy. Dani and my parents had come to see us off but Chiara became even more upset when she realised they weren't coming with us. She broke down crying. No Humphrey, no Nan, no 'Boss' and no Dani.

When the plane began to taxi, Chiara's tears made way for excitement. We were in a plane for the second time in six months which was quite an achievement for me. I'm terrified of flying. We arrived in Sydney less than two hours later. Sydney airport had flat escalators, like a conveyor belt for people. I was relieved not to have to carry Chiara for a long distance to collect our luggage and exit the terminal.

Driving via the tunnel under the Sydney harbour, the taxi driver didn't think to ask if any of us were claustrophobic. I hated it. What if we broke down? What if the tunnel collapsed under the stress of all that water? What if we can't get out for any reason at all? I was a nervous wreck by the time we arrived at the Catholic University on the North Shore, where we would spend the next four nights.

We were escorted to our room in the student boarding house, where on arrival I was informed that a Tutor had very kindly offered his room at short notice so we could stay with the group from Kensington. I didn't meet the Tutor to thank him personally, and I was feeling a little uncomfortable receiving such special treatment. I hoped he knew how much his kind gesture meant to us.

As I put Chiara into bed that night I talked to her about Mary MacKillop, and the reason we had travelled to Sydney. I told her that perhaps the 'come to me' in her dream was an invitation to be there so Mary could help her from heaven. I didn't mention that Mary MacKillop was a nun because Chiara wouldn't have understood what a nun was.

'Mummy, if Mary MacKillop cures me can I throw my tablets down the toilet?'

'Oh Chiara, of course you can darling. It would be good if she made you better, wouldn't it?'

'Yep it sure would.'

'Settle down now, and get some sleep. I'll see you in the morning.'

'Good night Mummy. I love you.'

'I love you too sweetheart.'

The tablets Chiara had referred to were Panadol she took for her pain, and the Phenobarbitone for her seizures. I wished Dani and my parents could have been in Sydney with us but without accommodation available it wasn't to be. I was worried about Chiara's level of pain, how she would behave for the five days and how I would cope, so far from home without any support. I continued to plead with Mary MacKillop, desperately wanting my little girl released from all her pain and suffering, and to regain the ability to speak, walk and behave normally again.

Chiara's almost constant screaming was an everyday challenge and I wondered if she was rebelling against everything life was throwing at her. I couldn't blame her if she was. With nothing to do in the room in Sydney but think, I invented the term 'Neuro Trauma.' It summed up the traumatic affect numerous neurosurgeries, hospital stays, scans, blood tests etc. had on Chiara's body, mind and soul. Those two words said it all, and from there I created the name for a support group I called SHUNT; Support for Hydrocephalus and Understanding Neurosurgical Trauma.

The next morning Chiara couldn't seem to wake up but I was confident she was okay. I was hungry but I wasn't going to leave her alone so I asked one of the ladies in the group to watch over her while I ran downstairs to get us both some breakfast. Everyone headed out for a day of sightseeing.

With two long days ahead I took Chiara to the local shopping centre instead. It wasn't long before she spotted a Lion King backpack and a dreaded screaming tantrum was in full swing with her demanding I buy it. Calming her down while being stared at by fellow customers, I told her if she behaved for the rest of our shopping trip I might buy her the backpack.

Sometimes disciplinary measures actually worked. We left the shopping centre with a smile on Chiara's face as wide as the Sydney Harbour Bridge. To see her face light up rather than so often grimacing in pain was worth whatever it took.

We travelled by bus the next day to an area known as the Domain to enjoy a concert organised to herald the Pope's arrival in Sydney. Many thousands of people were expected so we arrived early to secure good viewing positions. I dreaded spending eight long hours in one spot with a child prone to screaming and misbehaving. I was already drained at the thought but then realised, as I settled down beside her on a blanket on the ground, Chiara was remarkably calm.

She was sitting quietly playing with the toys I had packed in her new Lion King bag. I sat back to relax and enjoy the music, quietly thanking and crediting Mary MacKillop for soothing Chiara's behaviour, even if it was only temporary.

We spent Thursday at Randwick Racecourse for the beatification ceremony. The day involved sitting in a grandstand for six hours amongst strangers. I didn't need to worry about Chiara's behaviour because she was soon curled up on my lap sound asleep. Just as I thought she was going to sleep through the entire service, she woke up and together we watched the Pope beatify the Blessed Mary MacKillop.

We couldn't really hear what was being said and Chiara had no idea what was happening but it didn't matter. We were there, she was calm and I was constantly thanking Mary MacKillop for pacifying her and keeping her well while we were in Sydney. I felt we had already received a number of miracles along the way, and it was too greedy to beg, for more. So I prayed that if we couldn't have a cure, then could we *please* be granted five years' time-out so we could have a break long enough to re-energise our lives.

The next morning we were taken to Mary MacKillop's chapel at Marymount in North Sydney. At the front of the chapel near the altar, was Mary's tomb. We joined a long queue to enter the building, and for most of the time I was carrying Chiara on my hip.

When we walked through the door I stood approximately two metres back, unsure of how close we could get to the tomb without showing disrespect. Chiara started wriggling saying she wanted to get down so I sat her on the floor in front of me. All of a sudden she stood up holding on to me for stability then took my hand and pulled me towards the tomb.

After taking a few steps I whispered we were close enough and noticed Chiara seemed mesmerised, in a trance-like state. Instead of obeying me, she let go of my hand and slowly took a few steps, unaided, towards the tomb. It was weird but I sensed she was being beckoned closer. For the first time since the day of the rainbow incident in the hospital, I felt reassured Chiara would be okay. It was as though I was swathed in a veil of comfort and support. I can't explain the peculiar sensation.

As Chiara knelt almost on top of the beautiful marble tomb I started to rush forward to get her, thinking we'd be scolded by the nuns for impertinence. Just as I reached down to pick her up I caught sight of a nun out of the corner of my eye, and rather than scold us she gestured me to leave Chiara be.

Tears welled in my eyes as I acknowledged Chiara really *did* receive a personal invitation from Mary with the words in her dream, 'Come to me Chiara, come.' *This* is what she wanted! Chiara was where she was meant to be, kneeling at Mary's tomb. I had anguished over those words, thinking perhaps her message was to prepare me for the worst but all Mary MacKillop wanted was Chiara to visit her tomb. I was grappling to make sense of it all.

My baby girl had an apparent connection to Mary MacKillop but how did that ever come to be? We were on a mystifying journey. I began to reflect on my memories of attending Mary MacKillop College at Kensington when I was a teenager. I often felt drawn to a photo of Mary hanging on the wall at the bottom of the staircase. She was captivating and charismatic with soft warm eyes and a beautiful flawless face. Many years later, there I stood watching as my young daughter knelt transfixed at her tomb.

I felt completely absorbed in an aura of tranquillity when suddenly something flew out towards me. Jolting backwards in a reflex action I thought it must have been a bird. I hadn't seen a bird but I definitely saw something fly in front of my face. It happened again and that time I could see it wasn't a bird; it was letters flying out at me! No not letters, words! Words that grew larger the closer they came towards me! How was it possible to have words flying into my face?

It was truly bizarre and like watching a three dimensional movie, except we weren't in a movie theatre. I was sure I really was losing my mind but then realised the words were flying out from the end of the tomb. They were engraved in the marble yet flying out at me. I couldn't understand how it was possible. I became breathless, head spinning as I crumbled to the floor, at the same time trying to keep my eyes on Chiara.

Convinced I was going to pass out and end up in hospital leaving Chiara frightened and alone, I tried to alert someone to look after her but I couldn't speak or move. I hoped she wouldn't turn around to see me on the floor. Trying to get up I noticed someone was talking to me but I couldn't hear what she was saying.

'Are you alright dear?' I looked towards the voice. There was an elderly woman, concerned for my welfare, leaning over me.

'Yes I'm fine thank you.'

'Are you sure you're alright?'

'Yes,' I replied. 'It's just, it's just those words!'

'What words dear? What do you mean?'

'Those words. Those words there on the tomb.'

'Oh, *those* words dear, the words on the tomb that say Trust in God; that's what Mary MacKillop always said, trust in God. It was her favourite saying, so to speak.'

That's it! That's why we're here! Mary MacKillop has been with us all along and I never even realised! It must have been Mary's frustrated way of letting me know it was *her* whispering in my ear ever since the day my water broke. *'Trust in God Helen, trust in God.'*

I started babbling to the stranger. 'Mary MacKillop has been looking after us, I *know* that now! No wonder my daughter survived so much. Mary must have a special plan for her.' Confused at my gibberish the woman continued,

'Can I get you some water dear, you'd better come and sit down, you'll feel better then.'

'Oh I'm fine now, thank you. I'm here with my little girl she's over there kneeling at the tomb. We came because she dreamt of Mary MacKillop. It's all starting to make sense now. I'm sorry; you must think I'm crazy.' The old lady merely smiled at me.

Chiara was oblivious to what had happened. Eventually she moved and I went to help her up. I immediately noticed she appeared distinctively different. Taking my hand she whispered, 'We can go now mum.' Composed and placid, she was walking holding my hand and appeared to be at peace with herself. Her speech was clear and back to normal. I was astounded and thankful, not only at the fact she was walking and talking but at the difference in her overall demeanour and disposition.

Back on the bus we headed for Wonderland, an amusement park in Eastern Creek, to fill in a few hours before proceeding to the airport for the return flight home. Chiara was so chatty she had everyone laughing. After a long drive we arrived at Wonderland only to be turned away due to the inclement weather.

A group of disappointed children and accompanying adults agreed to visit the well-known tourist precinct known as The Rocks. A unique location beneath the Sydney Harbour Bridge with its rustic old-world buildings, it had a vibrant atmosphere and the shopping was irresistible.

By 3pm we were back at the airport. At the end of the departure lounge Chiara discovered a delightful play area complete with a maze. I hadn't seen her have so much fun since our trip to Queensland. When the announcement came over the public address system informing us our flight was ready to board, I called her to come out of the maze. 'No mum I don't want to go. I'm staying here.'

'Chiara you must get out now, the plane is leaving and we have to be on it or we won't get home.'

'No mum, you can tell them to wait. I want a bit longer this is great fun.'

Attempting to hide my exasperation while trying not to smile, I kept demanding she leave the maze. The more I tried, the more determined she was to stay but at least I knew it wasn't a behavioural problem, she was simply having fun manoeuvring through the equipment without help. When she emerged and I turned to collect our bags Chiara seized the opportunity and went back into the maze.

'If you want to stay here in the airport fine but I'm going home. The plane is leaving right now and I'm going to be on it with or without you. The pilot won't wait for you because all these people want to go home to their families and so do I. I'll tell everyone you didn't want to come home. I'm going now, goodbye.'

'Wait for *me* Mum. Wait for me!' she cried.

I was approximately three metres away and she ran up to me. We had arrived in Sydney with her struggling to walk and when she did, she had a wide gait, meaning her legs were wider apart than normal when she walked. Now, not only was she walking unaided but she ran the short distance to me. Floating high above the clouds heading home I was excited to think our lives might be about to get a whole lot easier.

When we were driving home from the airport Chiara asked, 'Mum can I throw my tablets down the toilet now? I'm all better. I don't feel sick anymore and my headache has gone. I don't want to take my tablets anymore.'

I was concerned what the repercussions would be taking her off the seizure medication. After a great deal of consideration, I agreed to wean her off the tablets. I was prepared to give her the opportunity to go without them.

While I was unpacking the car a neighbour came over to welcome us home followed by her six-year-old son. As we stood talking, Chiara and the young boy took off running down the street. 'Chiara don't go so faaaaar.'

'Oh my God. Look!'

'Helen what is it?'

'Look at Chiara. She can run and her wide gait seems to have improved. I can't believe she can run again. A week ago she could hardly walk or talk and now she's running and her legs are straight. Maybe going to the beatification *really* has helped. Isn't this exciting? Keep running Chiara, keep running but when you get to the end of the street come back!' I yelled.

At the age of seven she returned to school the first week of February 1995 ready to commence a new year. At the completion of the previous year we had a meeting where the teachers, deputy principal and I discussed concerns regarding schooling and her abilities.

Due to her health issues she had spent a great deal of time away from the classroom and as a result she was falling behind with her schoolwork. It was unanimously agreed that holding her back to repeat the year would be detrimental to her psychological well-being therefore she progressed into the next year level with extra help and support.

Teachers approached me at different times in the schoolyard with each asking the same question, 'What did you do over the holidays to bring on such a transformation in Chiara?' None of the teachers were aware of Chiara's dream or our trip to the beatification. My response to each of them simple, 'I guess we can thank Mary MacKillop.'

# *The flower girl*

On our return from Sydney I took out a loan and turned all my attention towards helping Dani plan her wedding, scheduled to take place eight weeks later. Mary MacKillop's chapel at St Joseph's Convent Kensington was the obvious preference for the ceremony. Dani, my precious little China Doll married Anthony on March 11, 1995 wearing a magnificent ivory raw silk gown complemented by matching headpiece of delicate silk roses and flowing veil. She looked absolutely stunning.

At 3pm the transport arrived in the shape of a dazzling sky-blue vintage Chevrolet. A second car arrived to ferry the bridesmaids but Chiara insisted on going with Dani and my father in the big blue Chevy. Driving slowly, it took almost an hour to travel the distance from our house to the chapel. Chiara fell asleep.

When the car parked, my brother Trevor lifted her out and handed her to me. I had to wake her so she could lead Dani and the bridesmaids down the aisle but she was still half asleep. She had been looking forward to her big sister's wedding and it appeared she would sleep through the ceremony. Dani, my father and the bridesmaids all waited patiently at the back of the chapel for her to wake up enough for her to join them.

I carried the sleepy flower girl and placed her in front of Dani, reminding her of the important role she was to play. I then took my place in the front pew with Robert - my friend who had lent me the laptop - and had accepted my invitation to partner me. The music began and Chiara was off, leading her big sister and the bridal party down the aisle. The picture perfect sight of my flawless Dani in her wedding gown about to be given away by my father, led by her brave young sister who only weeks before could only walk a few paces, triggered happy tears.

Halfway through the ceremony, the newlyweds sat to relax for a moment while music played softly in the background. Chiara saw them sit down and casually walked across to the other side of the chapel to give Dani a kiss and cuddle. The sight of her doing so, caused barely a dry eye to be found in the chapel. Everyone was aware of Chiara's time-bomb lifestyle and to see her doing so well after all she had been through was a joy to behold.

*Chiara the Flower girl*

With the service over, the photographer suggested the majestic convent gardens as an ideal setting for photos. Sister Margaret Lamb who helped arrange our beatification trip and accompanied us to Sydney, had taught Dani at school and recognised her name in the chapel's wedding register. While standing talking in the gardens enjoying the moment, Sister Margaret approached and asked me how Chiara was going and who was looking after her. 'What do you mean who's looking after her Sister, she's over there.'

'Where, I can't see her' she asked.

'Running around playing with all the other kids; she's the flower girl.'

'Don't tell me the adorable little flower girl is Chiara; it *can't* be. That's not the fragile child we took to Sydney only a few weeks ago who we all helped to carry! I can't believe she's running around and she looks really healthy. I would never have believed it without seeing her with my own eyes. What an incredible transformation.'

Grabbing my arm tightly, her eyes red, she held up a hand and with her fingers crossed continued,

'Could this be? Oh God, Helen, it's a miracle. There's no other explanation. I know what I saw in Sydney and how she struggled to walk and talk and how fragile she was. Oh, I hope this is our miracle, I'll keep all fingers crossed Helen.' Wiping tears from her face, unable to continue, she walked away shaking her head. She was hoping Chiara would be the second miracle the nuns and many Catholics of Australia had been waiting many years for.

# *Penola*

One month later with Chiara continuing to improve and no longer in pain, I decided to make the four-hour trip to Penola in the southeast to visit the school Mary MacKillop opened in 1867. I was seeking confirmation as to whether it was the same school Chiara saw in her dream.

While packing the car I mentioned to Chiara we were going to visit where Mary taught young children. I didn't mention the word 'schoolhouse' and still hadn't told her that Mary was a nun who wore a 'habit.' Chiara hadn't ever seen a nun in a habit as they generally wear casual clothing these days, as did the nuns who were with us in Sydney.

I wanted to see if Chiara would have any reaction if she saw a picture of Mary MacKillop or visited the place where Mary taught. She was familiar with priests in black clothing with their small white section in the front of their collar as she sometimes attended Church – which Catholics refer to as Mass – with my mother. I had arranged with my dearest friend Julie, for me to take her eight year old daughter Kimberlee with us so Chiara would have a play mate. Julie's older daughter Kylie was one of Dani's closest friends and now her younger daughter was one of Chiara's.

We stayed in a quaint, old-world cottage in Coonawarra a short distance from Penola, an area well known for its wine industry. I had planned for us to visit the schoolhouse the following day. The girls loved the old cottage so much they asked if we could stay for a *really* long holiday. Having too much fun to go to bed, I allowed them to stay up to finish their games. I was feeling tired so I went to lie down.

Chiara appeared at the side of the bed and I asked what she wanted. 'I want to get up into your big bed but I can't cos it's too high.' In typical Chiara style no sooner had I helped her settle beneath the thick feathery doona she said,

'See ya mum I'm going back to Kimberlee now. I just wanted to try out your bed.'

The next morning we drove to Penola. As I parked the car, both the girls, wide-eyed simultaneously asked, 'Is that the *whole* school?'

'Yes girls. It's the whole school.'

'Wow,' said Chiara as they both ran off leaving me to close their doors and lock the car. Kimberlee ran on ahead and sat inside at a table where she began drawing. Chiara stood motionless in the doorway. I moved so I could see her face as she entered the building then followed in behind her. I didn't know what to expect and whether we'd be able to go inside so I was surprised to see the room was still set up as a classroom from the 1800s. I noticed Chiara was scanning the room. Moving slowly, she paused to look at very old photos on the wall. She recognised them as priests, by their white collar inserts. 'Mummy isn't that Father Paul?' she asked pointing to a particular priest.

'Father who?'

'You know mum, Father Paul.'

'Chiara, I don't know a Father Paul.'

'Oh mum,' she sighed, 'of course you do.' She then continued, 'Mum we know most of these people don't we.' Feeling slightly bemused I said, 'Well you might know them but I'm afraid I don't.' She continued to scan each photo on the board asking questions about some of the people. I was at a loss to answer. She then moved away to look through old letters, books, and pictures.

Other visitors were beginning to notice her presence in the room. One of the caretaker women who I presumed to be a nun, came over and said, 'Excuse me I've been watching your little girl, she's obviously been here before.'

'No she hasn't. None of us have why do you ask?'

'Well I don't know what it is but there's definitely something special going on here. I can't explain it. Are you sure she hasn't been before, perhaps with someone else? Watching the way she's conducting herself, engrossed in everything is very different to any other child I've seen visit here. I thought she must've been before. Tell me, is there a story here?'

'Is it *that* obvious?' I asked.

'Yes it is. Can I ask you to please tell me, I'd really love to know?'

'Sure, I don't mind sharing Chiara's story but I'm not sure you will believe it. I grapple with it myself and I've lived it with her!'

'Oh I'll believe it. I can see something amazing in your little girl that I've never seen before.' I gave the woman a brief outline of Chiara's history, her dream and our reason for visiting Penola. As I was speaking others gathered around to listen.

'Thank you so much for telling us Chiara's story. You've certainly been on an extraordinary journey. I think it's really important for people to share their stories, otherwise how would we ever know.'

'Well, funny you should say that because I was asked to write a book about her life when she was four years old. Since then I've thought it was finished a few times but things keep happening with her, so the book keeps writing itself as we live it. I don't know when it will ever be finished because I keep adding to it like a journal.'

She smiled. 'I'll look forward to reading your book.'

I laughed and said, 'Well don't hold your breath because I don't know if it will ever get finished. I don't even know what the final chapter will be about so it may never be published.'

Chiara spotted a huge oil painting hanging high up on the wall. The painting was of a woman wearing a green dress. I presumed it was Mary MacKillop when she was young. 'That's not Mary MacKillop is it mum?'

'I beg your pardon Chiara what did you say?'

'I said that's *not* Mary MacKillop.'

'What do you mean it's not? I don't think it would be up there if it wasn't.'

'It just isn't her, mum.'

Everyone momentarily stopped to look up at the painting without uttering a sound. Then one of the nuns came over and whispered, 'That's three thousand dollars' worth of painting, what does your daughter mean it's not Mary MacKillop?'

'I'm sorry, I don't know. I'll talk to her.'

'Chiara why are you saying the painting isn't Mary MacKillop?'

'Because it isn't Mum. I know the painting isn't her.'

'But *how* do you know? How can you be so sure it isn't Mary?'

Exasperated she continued, 'Well look at the eyes. They're *not* Mary's eyes, her eyes aren't like that.' Another woman approached, 'Chiara why do you think that painting isn't Mary MacKillop?'

'I know it isn't Mary because I've seen her and she doesn't look like that, her face is different' she responded.

Chiara walked across to a photograph on a window-sill. In the photo Mary is dressed in her nun's habit. Chiara carefully picked it up and announced, 'See, look, *this* is Mary MacKillop in this photo. That's her, that's who I saw!' She then placed the photo back on the window-sill and moved away. I was astounded when I realised what had happened. Chiara had gone straight to a photo of a nun wearing a habit and casually proclaimed, *that* was Mary MacKillop; she recognised her as the person in her dream!

I picked up the photo and studied her eyes. Holding out the photo I gasped, 'Look at this!'

'What, what is it?' a lady asked.

'Look at the eyes! Maybe Chiara's right. The eyes are different. In the photo her eyes are peaceful and warm but in the painting they're cold and lifeless and the shape of her face is different. I appreciate it's a superb painting but is it supposed to be Mary MacKillop? People were peering over my shoulder, glancing at the photo.

The old building was chilly so one of the women went to get a log of wood. As she bent down to poke the fire Chiara went up to her and putting an arm on the woman's shoulder said, 'I see you still have the fireplace.'

'Pardon what did you say?' the woman asked.

'I said I see you still have the fireplace.'

Looking up from the book I was reading, I saw a pair of eyes glaring straight at me. 'I thought you said your daughter hasn't been here before.'

'She hasn't,' I said. Chiara continued. 'I see the blackboard is in the same place too.' My eyes practically popped out of my head. 'Chiara, what did you just say?'

'I said the fireplace is in the same place and so is the blackboard.' I couldn't speak.

'Chiara you've been here before, haven't you?' asked an obviously very confused woman.

'No I haven't,' she replied.

'Well then, why are you saying the fireplace and the blackboard are in the same place?'

'Because I saw them in my dream.'

'What dream?' the woman asked.

'The dream when I saw Mary MacKillop. She was standing here in this little schoolhouse and I saw the fireplace and the blackboard in my dream too. I just remember seeing them, that's all.'

Chiara ran off to join Kimberlee who was still sitting at the antiquated wooden table, drawing with chalk on a small, old-fashioned slate tablet. The longer we were there the more I became consumed with attempting to process *how* our lives had become entwined with Mary MacKillop. I hoped to identify a reason.

As much as I sensed we belonged there and wanted to stay, I was aware some people in the room were understandably suspicious about us claiming we'd never been there before, so I went to collect the girls to leave. Chiara moved the chair out from the table and I saw she had written on her little chalk slate the words, 'Please Mary MacKillop cuu (sic) me.'

*The Schoolhouse Penola*

My heart aching I wanted to promise she *would* be cured. I was surprised at her spelling, particularly as she spelt MacKillop correctly but not cure. I picked up the slate and showed the nun. 'Look what Chiara has written!'

'That's so special, don't rub it off we'll keep it for everyone to see.'

We said our goodbyes and made our way across to the chapel where I was invited to put Chiara's name and brief details in the special intentions book. By doing so she would be prayed for in a mass held every Wednesday that is specifically for anyone afflicted with illness and suffering.

After spending time in the chapel we went to the local bakery for lunch then headed home. My head was spinning. I was intrigued by the incomprehensible events that had unfolded, and pleased there were others who witnessed it. Chiara's natural response in the schoolhouse left me in no doubt; she truly belonged in the world of Mary MacKillop.

# *Visions continue*

On December 28, 1995 Chiara experienced yet another 'visit' from Jason. A visit different to any she had previously, leaving me disconcerted. Opening her eyes she casually said, 'Mummy I saw Jason again last night.'

'Did you darling? Did he speak to you?'

'Yes, he said he came to show me a place.'

'What do you mean a place?'

'He said he came to take me, to show me, a place.' Not knowing what it meant I gazed into her eyes and nervously asked, 'So did he?'

'Yes he did. He took me and we sort of flew. There was this black thing sort of like a black tunnel that had a light at the end of it and we sort of went through, then we flew to a house high up in the sky on top of the trees. Jason knocked on the door but no-one answered and I got sick of waiting. I was really scared so I climbed back down the tree and when I got to the bottom I looked up and saw an old man answer the door. Jason went inside. I was really scared mum, there were dead people inside. I was crying cos I was very frightened and couldn't find my way home. Then Jason was next to me and he asked why I was crying. I told him I couldn't find my way home. He said, 'don't cry

Chiara you are home. You are at the house next door, see there's your house and then he pointed to our house.'

'But if you already climbed down the tree how did you know there were dead people inside the house' I asked.

'Because I just knew.'

'What happened then, did he say or do anything else?'

'Oh he just said he'll take me there again one day.' I asked whether she was scared the whole time and she said, 'No, not all the time only when I knew there were dead people in the house and I couldn't find my way home.'

That visit took place on the 18th anniversary of Jason's passing. I spent the day depressed and teary, unable to function. I couldn't stop worrying about what his visit might have meant. On numerous occasions over the years when Chiara hadn't been well she would say, 'It's okay Mum, Jason's here.' I always experienced a sense of peace when she said that but this visit left me disillusioned. Was he preparing Chiara, and warning me?

# *From celebrations to commiserations*

One Saturday afternoon in October 1998 a girlfriend Gill rang and suggested we go to see a movie. Chiara was staying with my parents for the night so when we left the cinema we decided to go to a hotel for a few drinks before parting ways and heading home. It was at the hotel that I met Steve.

We chatted the night away until the hotel closed and he invited me back to his house for coffee. When I left he asked for my phone number and rang me the next morning at 9am to arrange to see me again. We quickly became inseparable and Chiara was thrilled to have him in our lives. It wasn't long before I polished up my secretarial skills and joined his television production business as company Secretary. It was a complete change of lifestyle and I thoroughly enjoyed it in between hospital stays with Chiara.

Mid-December, six weeks after our first meeting, on bended knee Steve proposed. I wasn't keen because of all the heartache and few violent relationships I had experienced in the past. I suggested he ask again in six months. Commitment shy, I wasn't ready to chance more misery. Before too long we were happily living together.

In February 1999 I was delighted to become a grandparent to Dani's first precious child. Braeden Louis was proudly placed into my arms as Chiara rejoiced at becoming a doting aunty.

Six months later, with a successful business and finances vastly improving, we bought a beach house in a small fishing town on the Yorke Peninsula, two hours north of Adelaide. We could spend as much time as we wanted at the beach every weekend, school holidays and whenever we could manage in between hospital trips and television production contracts. Chiara was very excited when Steve bought a boat and she quickly discovered a love of fishing. She talked him into taking her out in the boat as often as possible.

Life was close to perfect as we entered a new phase together with Steve obviously counting down the months, proposing again and that time I didn't hesitate. With his two young children, Cassie and Aaron living with us from time to time, we began construction of our two-storey five bedroom, three bathroom dream home at Gulfview Heights. We also built a storage facility for the television production trucks and equipment at an industrial site nearby in Golden Grove.

*Chiara loves fishing age 13yrs*

We set our wedding date for 15 April 2000. Within weeks we were approached to cover a television event in New South Wales that same weekend. We would need numerous staff over a five-day period, paying not only their wages but flights, accommodation and meals as well as living away from home allowances, and fuel for our three outside broadcast vehicles, on top of our own expenses.

It was an exciting assignment but intuition struck and something didn't feel right so I convinced Steve to request half the payment up front or we wouldn't be accepting the massive contract. He was reluctant and said it wasn't the way things were done in the television industry. He eventually agreed to ask, and the event organiser surprisingly agreed to make an upfront payment. Wedding invitations hadn't been printed so we changed the date to accommodate the event, and as promised half the fee was paid into our bank account.

We brought our wedding date forward one week and married 8 April 2000 in a lovely scenic garden setting with my friend Julie, Dani and Chiara as Bridesmaids, and Braeden just toddling, was the cute little pageboy. Steve's then nine-year-old daughter Cassie was junior bridesmaid and his four-year-old son Aaron took his place at his father's side along with the groomsmen.

The ceremony was followed by a relaxed reception. It was the tonic we all needed, a world away from the stress of hospitals and surgeries. Married in the Catholic Church in 1973, as much as I would have preferred another Church wedding, I deemed it hypocritical.

My first marriage would have to be annulled which I wasn't prepared to do, given my beautiful Dani was born as a result of that union. During wedding preparations we discovered Dani was pregnant with her second child and five months later I was blessed with an adorable grand-daughter Tayah Marie giving me two perfect, healthy cherubs to enjoy.

Without time for a honeymoon and with Chiara holidaying at my parents we set off to New South Wales a few days after our wedding, to cover the four day event. On completion, our television coverage was hailed a complete success which was a relief being such a mammoth production to undertake. We sent our staff home on their pre-booked

From celebrations to commiserations 201

*Helen and Steve 2000*

*Helen and Chiara*

*With my parents Allan and Laurel on my wedding day*

flights and organised to meet our truck drivers for an overnight stay at a motel in Hay, half-way home.

As we drove to the exit gate on the Monday, Steve recognised the event organiser walking towards us. He stopped to chat to him. When their conversation ended I told Steve the man's demeanour didn't seem right and he said I was imagining it, that he was probably just glad it was over. I suspected there was more to it than that. We arrived in Hay, bought pizzas and drinks for our truck drivers, held a debrief, and then retired early.

The next morning approximately an hour into our trip home Steve's mobile phone rang. It was one of our industry colleagues who had also been contracted to work on the event we had just finished. He rang to say he'd heard on good authority that the gate takings didn't cover the expenses that the organiser had gone into voluntary liquidation, and therefore no one would be paid.

With his gut churning, Steve rang our truck drivers asking them to meet us at a hotel on the northern outskirts of Adelaide, where we dropped the bombshell. We promised that even though it would probably sink our business, they and the rest of our crew would all receive their full entitlements.

Although we had received half the payment up front it only covered part of the expenses, and we used our last cent paying wages, allowances, meals, flights and accommodation for all staff members. I was surprised how placid Steve was, quietly managing all the drama that had swiftly and unexpectedly impacted our lives.

# *Mary MacKillop's second miracle*

In 2000, soon after marrying Steve, I was contacted by Sister Margaret, the nun who organised our travel to Sydney for the beatification. She told me that after she witnessed Chiara's transformation at Dani's wedding, she had contacted the relevant people regarding the possibility of Chiara being deemed Mary MacKillop's second miracle. I was confused as to how Chiara could be the person the nuns needed, given the fact that she wasn't cured.

It was explained to me a miracle didn't necessarily have to involve a cure. Chiara still might qualify but there was a long road ahead and many people would need to be interviewed. This led to a chain of events, including meeting Father Paul Gardiner, and welcoming him, Sister Margaret and others who were representing the Vatican, into our home. They presented Chiara with a Relic of Mary MacKillop which was a small photo of Mary, approximately one inch square (2.5 cm) with a tiny white piece of Mary's clothing attached to it.

I still hadn't told anyone about the whispering voice I had heard over the years, or the words that flew towards me from the tomb. I agreed to have Chiara's case put forward based solely on her 'vision' and sudden recovery. I wasn't convinced I wanted my daughter proclaimed the second miracle, especially when she was too young at the time to understand and have a say.

*A relic of Mary MacKillop*

On meeting Father Paul my mind reflected back to the scene in the schoolhouse where Chiara was looking at the photo of the priests on the wall, adamant I knew Father Paul. Until the day he entered our home I had never met a priest of that name. I presume it was nothing more than a co-incidence.

After decades of prayers, the Josephite nun's cause, was rapidly gaining momentum for the Pope to acknowledge a second Australian miracle directly attributed to Mary MacKillop. The first, a young woman aged twenty three and only married for two years in the 1960s was diagnosed with acute myeloblastic leukaemia. She was given no hope of survival and consequently sent home to die from the Mater Hospital located in North Sydney.

Doctors were astounded when her leukaemia suddenly disappeared and she made a complete recovery after the nuns had prayed to Mary MacKillop for a cure, on her behalf. The woman went on to give birth to six healthy children. The miracle was eventually verified by the Vatican in 1993 which lead to the beatification of Mary MacKillop in 1995 but there still needed to be another recognised miracle before Mary could be canonised a saint.

I began to agonise over what it would mean to us and our future if my young daughter was declared the second miracle. We had enough to cope with and I didn't need confirmation of Chiara's miracles. It would take many years before a decision would be made. Meanwhile Chiara's principal doctors were interviewed and all confirmed they couldn't explain her transformation – medically or scientifically – since the beatification.

# The Novena

Chiara was offered a scholarship at the age of thirteen, enabling her to attend Mary MacKillop College at Kensington. As we looked forward to our first family Christmas together, with Steve and his two children, Dani and grand-children, Chiara began complaining about her eyesight. I presumed it was a problem for the eye specialist to diagnose.

Dr Pater discovered swelling behind her eyes and suggested we see Mr Hanieh as a matter of urgency. An MRI scan revealed she had three cysts in her brain stem again. Mr Hanieh, reluctant to touch them, advised us to return for another check in three months. I was concerned that he didn't book surgery immediately and worried what effect waiting would have.

After ten weeks, Chiara was lethargic, not eating or talking. All she wanted to do was sleep. We returned to the hospital for another MRI that didn't reveal any changes. Mr Hanieh said he could operate but it was clear he was reluctant to do so. Chiara told him she didn't want any more surgery, and respecting her wishes, we left his office and returned home. Chiara was now old enough to have a say in her future treatment and she stood determined. I supported her decision but felt gutted not knowing how to help, as I watched her fade each day.

I kept in contact with the principal of Mary MacKillop College, so he knew what was going on with Chiara's health and consequent school absence. He asked if the college could offer a Novena to Mary MacKillop in the hope of receiving another miracle. Believing a Novena was only conducted for those without hope I was hesitant to accept, as hope was all I had left to cling to.

In desperation I agreed to meet him to discuss what was involved. I took Chiara to my parent's house as she was too ill to attend with me. At the conclusion of the meeting I wanted to digest what a Novena entailed so I walked across the road to the chapel, and sat gazing at a photo of Mary MacKillop. I felt defeated. There was no doubt in my mind she had been looking after us but I questioned how much more could I ask of her. I wondered what Mr Hanieh wasn't telling me. He was hesitating to operate. But why?

As I sat reflecting, I remembered pleading with Mary MacKillop at the beatification, for a five year break from Chiara's suffering. It was then I suddenly realised our five years had already expired. I left the chapel mentally drained, blaming myself for not asking for a lifetime of no more surgery, not just five short years.

It took a few days to find the courage to agree to the Novena. I had to accept the harsh reality that *we* were without hope. While I applauded the offer of help, I was overwhelmed knowing it probably meant hundreds of people, the majority of whom had never heard of Chiara, taking time out of their day to say special prayers for my youngest child, every day, for nine consecutive days. I granted permission to proceed, admitting it was Chiara's only chance as she was deteriorating every day. I was afraid I was losing her.

A Novena requires precise organisation. The school principal immediately contacted the nuns in Sydney to have the Novena commenced by as many people as possible. A few weeks later it began and I too prayed for the nine days necessary to achieve a positive outcome. Each day I watched for the slightest change but by the ninth day the Novena had run its course, and after hoping, praying and begging, I became deeply depressed when there wasn't any improvement. I felt embarrassed at having wasted everyone's time.

Early in the afternoon on the tenth day both Steve and I were shocked when Chiara muttered a few words while lying on the couch. She hadn't spoken in weeks. I tried not to get excited, and fobbed it off as a coincidence. If Steve hadn't heard her too I would have thought I imagined it. Getting her to eat had been an everyday battle as she didn't have an appetite. The next day she said she was hungry.

On the twelfth day she was up running around as though nothing had happened. She returned to school the next day. I was amazed and relieved. The Novena must have worked! Some would say it was coincidental and perhaps it was but I didn't care. She had been very ill, in terrible pain, not moving or talking, and barely eating for many weeks.

Then ten days after the Novena started, she began to show improvement and by the twelfth day was healthy again. How to thank each person who took part was foremost on my mind. Without the means to do so, I hoped Chiara's story, along with our eternal gratitude, will someday find its way to at least one person who helped us. I want them to know how extremely appreciative I am.

We attended Chiara's follow-up appointment with the eye specialist to check on the swelling behind her eyes a few weeks later. As he examined her he exclaimed, 'I don't believe this.' I asked what was wrong. 'She didn't end up having surgery did she?' he asked.

'No she hasn't yet. Mr Hanieh seems reluctant to operate for some reason. Why?'

'Well, the swelling; it's gone! I can't explain it. I absolutely can't explain it. I expected it to be worse by now without surgery. She definitely had a lot of swelling when I last saw her and I was certain she would need surgery but now it's gone!'

'Well that's really strange,' I said, 'because Mr Hanieh ordered an MRI after you sent us back to him and it showed she had three cysts in her brain stem which explains the swelling you saw. All I know is, she's certainly better now.'

Chiara smiled. 'I can explain it.' She proceeded to tell him all about Mary MacKillop. Dr Pater looked at me sideways, 'Mary MacKillop eh? Well Chiara, something has definitely happened here that I can't explain.' Hearing his words, wiped away any doubt the Novena had worked. The cysts had miraculously disappeared without surgical intervention. A follow up MRI confirmed the cysts were no longer present.

# *Our world explodes*

By the end of 2001 we had enough contracts for our television production business to see us through to the completion of our new home and storage facility. Conscious of the fact that digital television at that time was due to begin in 2008, we had set up a solid five-year business plan in 1998 to take us through to 2003. It would enable us to have a five-year buffer before the digital switchover would hail the demise of our analogue business and give us time to decide on our future thereafter.

In early 2002, with mortgages on our home, storage facility and business equipment, the television industry began demanding production and archiving of material in digital format, six years earlier than anticipated. Without two million dollars to enable us to advance to digital equipment and coupled with the financial setback in 2000, it was impossible for us to continue the business.

Two years had passed since the Novena. Chiara once again began experiencing excruciating headaches daily so I made an appointment with Mr Hanieh. She had an MRI that determined the shunt in her fourth ventricle had blocked.

It was 11 July 2002, Chiara's fifteenth birthday. Due to complications she underwent neurosurgery three times in a twenty-four-hour period and admitted into the Intensive Care Unit. She was lying on her left side, and while I was talking to her, I realised she couldn't hear me. Mr Hanieh couldn't offer any explanation for her sudden hearing loss. He seemed distant and vague and appeared to be looking straight through me. I was as concerned about him as I was for Chiara. Something was wrong. I had never seen him look like that before.

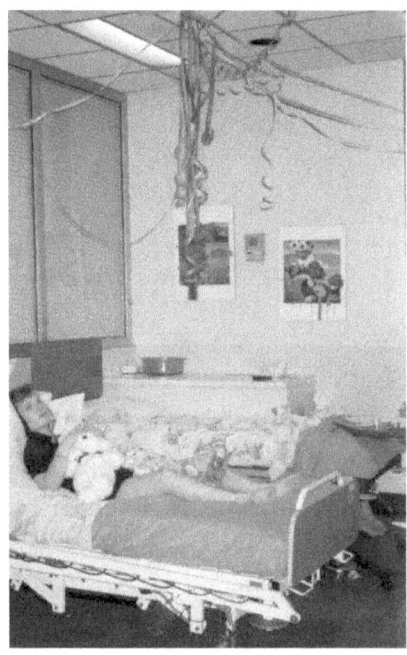

*Chiara undergoes Neurosurgery for the 50th time on her 15th Birthday*

When she recovered, Mr Hanieh sent us to an ear specialist who determined her hearing was irreparably damaged. He mentioned she could have a cochlear implant if she lost the hearing in her left ear in the future. Chiara took the news in her stride but I was devastated for her.

On August 30 2002 Dani handed me baby Jai Joseph, happily sucking a blue dummy. He was the third precious, healthy grandchild to join our family. I was deliriously happy with three gorgeous grandchildren to love, and of course spoil.

Chiara and I returned to the Women's and Children's Hospital Outpatients ward to see Mr Hanieh for Chiara's six-week post-operative check-up. Reading magazines in the waiting room I overheard a man say in a jovial voice, 'Mr Hanieh's gone AWOL.' (A term used in the Armed Forces meaning, Absent Without Leave).

I presumed he must have been called to an emergency and would be late, so we sat patiently waiting for him to return. Chiara's name was called and we were led into a room we'd been in numerous times before to see Mr Hanieh. The doctor sitting at the desk casually mentioned Mr Hanieh had left and wouldn't be returning. I was distraught at the thought of losing the most important, and much loved member of our medical support team.

He was our world. How could I ever trust anyone else to look after Chiara? It took every ounce of my being not to break down and burst into tears. I was gutted. It was only a couple of months prior to this that he and I had a conversation about his retirement. He reassured me he had no intention of retiring for at least a few more years.

*Our beautiful special friend, Mr Hanieh on Chiara's 15th Birthday at the Women's and Children's Hospital. Unbeknown to us at the time, this would be the last time we'd see him.*

The doctor didn't say it but I assumed Mr Hanieh wasn't there because he must have taken ill. Chiara was visibly upset and confused as to why Mr Hanieh wasn't seeing her. Our world had suddenly and unexpectedly exploded with our most significant support person no longer there for us. I was extremely worried about what had happened to him. He was my pillar of strength and encouragement, my sanity, champion and hero. In his own words, Chiara was 'One of the prizes of the profession' and she was very special to him, and he to her. He was best friend, comrade, rescuer, and saviour, our everything. I tried to find out what had happened but no-one would tell me.

Without warning and without planning, Chiara's medical and surgical future was thrown into jeopardy with him gone from our lives forever. Never again would we see the man with the beautiful face and brilliant mind. An extraordinary neurosurgeon, a man we loved so dearly. I didn't know what to do. Mr Hanieh could never be replaced. We'd never recover from losing such a remarkable man even though it was inevitable someday he'd retire.

It is with the utmost gratification we had Mr Hanieh throughout Chiara's childhood years. Words cannot describe how it felt every time I had to call on him especially in the middle of the night, and without question or hesitation, he was there, regardless of the hour. He never entertained the thought of giving up. She was one of many of his patients, and from what I saw he treated all children and their parents with the same respect he afforded us.

If it were not for Mr Hanieh and his unrelenting faith in Chiara, and recognition of my intuition as her mother, she may have been denied her extraordinary journey, her visions, and a life entwined with Mary MacKillop's miracles. Thank God for Mr Hanieh!

# Changing doctors and direction

With Mr Hanieh no longer available to treat Chiara I was informed she would automatically be 'taken over' by another neurosurgeon and transferred to the Royal Adelaide Hospital when she turned eighteen. Private health insurance enabled us to have the privilege of choosing an entire new team from the pool of South Australian surgeons and specialists who could continue Chiara's care. I refused to accept the proposal of another neurosurgeon and hospital before I had researched all available options.

Whether Chiara continued in the public or private system was irrelevant, I just had to find the best team that she would accept. The decision on a hospital would depend on where the team we chose consulted. As a matter of urgency I sought to find another neurosurgeon, neurologist and physician to have Chiara covered in case of emergency.

My trusted intuition kicked in the moment I met Dr Nik Vrodos, and when he agreed to accept Chiara as his neurosurgical patient I arranged for her to meet him. I was relieved to hear she liked Dr Vrodos too. With her neurosurgeon established I then concentrated on finding a neurologist and physician. I subsequently learned that all of the three chosen specialists not only know each other but communicate and consult together, confirming I found the best possible crew.

Meanwhile, Chiara often became disoriented at high school. She would become confused and upset as she tried to find her way to all the different classrooms. Primary school had been easier because they stayed in the one classroom. Chiara wasn't coping with the demands of school and the stress caused her excruciating headaches on a daily basis. In mid-2003, with her health of paramount concern I made an appointment with the school principal and her doctors to discuss the best way forward. Chiara was eager to continue at school but was in terrible pain and had difficulty hearing the teachers.

By this time I had to accept that the doctors at the Queen Victoria Hospital were correct when they warned me - when Chiara was a tiny baby - that she would never be able to grasp mathematics. She had also now been formally diagnosed with the Cerebral Palsy I had been warned about and a mild intellectual disability which often caused her frustration and confusion trying to understand commands placed on her, making it too difficult to stay at school.

Her health had to take priority over her education. It was a difficult decision but with the Principal, teachers and doctors all in agreement, she left school half way through year nine. The daily headaches and stress soon disappeared confirming the decision was the right one.

***

With our business now worthless due to the demise of analogue television, we were unemployed, without an income but still had debts to pay. We were left without any alternative but to sell our beautiful new home and storage facility, and move into our beach house. Fortunately it had appreciated enough in value that the bank allowed us to borrow against it to clear most of the outstanding debts but it left us penniless.

I was eventually granted the Carer Payment and Allowance for Chiara and we were grateful that Steve was fortunate to soon gain casual employment with an electrician but due to him having an income, I only received a small portion of the Commonwealth payments. It wasn't enough to pay the bills, so with insufficient income we lived the credit card merry-go-round that I called 'rent-a-life.' We were struggling financially and Chiara's persistent health issues now required a five-hour round trip to Adelaide for appointments and hospital admissions.

Quickly becoming part of our new community, I accepted the volunteer position of President of the Progress Association which worked to improve the aesthetics and maintenance of our town. I enjoyed the challenge, and as it was voluntary, although I often worked seven days a week, it enabled me to do so from home while continuing my daily care for Chiara, working around hospital trips and her ill health. I held the position for approximately ten years before retiring in 2014.

By 2004 Dani's irreconcilable marriage had run its course. She became a single parent with three young children to care for. She shared equal custody with her ex-husband. I worried about them every minute of every day because I wasn't close by to help if they needed me. I was relieved when she entered a new relationship with a long term friend of hers.

In 2005 Steve was fortunate to gain full time employment with the local council. His new job helped to improve the finances slightly but not enough to clear the debt as my Carer payment was further reduced as his income increased. Our financial merry-go-round continued.

# Flinders Medical Centre Adelaide

In October 2007 Chiara underwent surgery for endometriosis and within a few weeks she was complaining of stomach pain in the middle of her abdomen that moved to the right or left side of her pelvis, and sometimes was on both sides. When she became irritable, saying bizarre things at random, it was apparent something peculiar was developing. I took her to a local doctor but because she wasn't rambling or in a great deal of pain at the time, I couldn't convince him she was ill. We were back to playing the waiting game once again. She would either get better or worse, only time would tell.

The pain continued to fluctuate and by late December she was occasionally complaining of pain in her side. I kept insisting we revisit the doctor but she refused, saying they couldn't do anything to help her and the pain would go away. At twenty years of age, an adult with the right to make her own decisions, she was morphing into her sister!

Dani rarely took ill, so visits to the doctor usually meant traumatic vaccination injections. She was terrified of needles and could be very stubborn refusing to go to the doctor because it usually only ever meant a dreaded injection. Now Chiara was showing the same traits as her sister and it proved very frustrating and distressing for me. I just wanted to pick her up, put her in the car and go but she was too heavy by then for me to lift her. I respected her decision but monitored her closely. I knew it was only a matter of time.

On a trip back from Adelaide after visiting my parents, Chiara was behaving completely out of character. She talked incessantly, constantly changing the subject. It was difficult not to lose patience and tell her to keep quiet. I was trying to concentrate on driving on the country road.

Desperate for a diagnosis for Chiara's pain and strange behaviour, even though she protested, I managed to take her back to the doctor to get an urgent referral to her physician. I was worried about what was evolving with her health.

On Monday 21 January 2008 she lost her balance and injured her ankle. It wasn't a simple stumble. Whatever was wrong, she was deteriorating rapidly. Friends were beginning to comment that she didn't look well. I was sitting at the computer when she came to me terrified, declaring there were maggots coming out of her. Horror-struck we rushed back to the doctor. He was perplexed why she said such a weird thing. As she appeared normal he sent us home aware that we had an appointment to see the physician in Adelaide - a five hour round trip - the next day.

Soon after arriving home Chiara asked to use the computer. As she sat down she told me excitedly that she had 'made Broadband.' I asked her to repeat what she said. 'I've made Broadband Mum, quick come and have a look. I've done it, I've made Broadband.' I couldn't recognise the symptoms of whatever was manifesting. I was frightened.

At 1am next morning she was knocking on her bedroom wall excitedly saying she'd made a cocoon. When I went into her room I found her wide-eyed sitting on the bed. She looked strange. I calmly suggested she get some sleep as it was very late. I was confident the physician would discover the cause of whatever was going on, at our appointment the next day. Knocking loudly on the wall again she told me she had 'built a cubby house' (which of course she hadn't). I crawled into bed with her, accepting I wouldn't be getting any sleep.

At 3am she let out a blood curdling scream and shaking violently it was clear she was being terrorised. Incoherent she was babbling about the neighbour's door and ants and maggots crawling all over her, while alternating between grabbing her head and then stomach. She was annoyed because I couldn't see the ants or maggots and it dawned on me she was hallucinating and in terrible pain. I screamed for Steve who was asleep to come and sit with her. That man would sleep through an earthquake.

I rang triple 0 for an ambulance, and called back twice more panic-stricken. We were taken to the local hospital and admitted as she started flicking invisible ants from her ears and face. I asked the attending doctor to contact her neurosurgeon urgently to arrange a transfer to the Flinders Medical Centre in Adelaide where she could be assessed. The doctor returned saying there weren't any beds available and she'd have to go to the Royal Adelaide Hospital. I knew it was useless protesting even though I worried that no-one knew us at the Royal Adelaide.

The Royal Flying Doctor flew us to Adelaide and we arrived at 5am. With Chiara's complex medical history of which the doctor's had no knowledge, I asked for her to be transferred to Dr Vrodos at Flinders Medical Centre. I stated I'd take full responsibility for my decision.

The doctors at the Royal Adelaide Hospital asked whether I thought Chiara was acting normally. 'No,' I answered exasperated, 'she appears to have suddenly gone insane. She's hallucinating and in tremendous pain in her head and abdomen.' The doctors agreed to transfer her. After waiting for twelve hours to be transferred, I reached the stage where I was about to tell them to admit her into the Royal Adelaide Hospital as she desperately needed help. By chance the same ambulance officers who had collected us from the airport returned to take us to Flinders. They immediately recognised how much she had deteriorated in those hours, and refused to do so without a doctor on board. No doctors were available to accompany us in the ambulance.

With Chiara rapidly deteriorating they were forced to take us without medical support. By that time, both her hands and arms were simultaneously moving in a mirror image then changed to one arm relaxing, and the other moving and stiffening. The doctors made comment of it but didn't explain what it meant. All throughout, Chiara acknowledged questions but her answers were mostly muddled.

Dani arrived at Flinders Medical Centre soon after we did. Chiara recognised her and knew that I was her mother but couldn't remember our names, or her own, and was incoherent. Distraught, I was convinced my daughter would die without immediate help. I continually begged for help but no-one seemed overly concerned.

I kept asking for Dr Vrodos to be contacted because he would immediately recognise how ill she was. I told the staff something had gone very wrong with her brain. I repeatedly requested an MRI scan or an EEG, or both. A female nurse was angry because Chiara wouldn't co-operate while she tried to check her pupils. It was obvious to me that Chiara couldn't stand the light in her eyes.

The male nurse, who was assigned to her, accused her of pretending to be ill because he couldn't find anything wrong. 'Oh I know *exactly* what's going on here. There's more to this than meets the eye. She *only* co-operates when she wants to, there's nothing wrong with her. Haven't you seen the movie, *'Don't say a word?*' I could have punched him! He left the room and never returned.

Mortified, I asked Dani if she had heard of the movie and she told me it was about a young girl who pretended to be mentally ill. It was our first experience at the Flinders Medical Centre Emergency Department. I had made a terrible mistake insisting she be transferred there on that occasion. A decision I have to live with and will never forgive myself for, not having her admitted into the Royal Adelaide Hospital when we first arrived there.

Several hours later a doctor appeared who asked questions and carefully listened to my answers. At last someone was showing an interest. He noticed the unusual hand movements and asked if it was normal. I was in tears, frustrated and exhausted, and told him, 'No, nothing about her is normal at the moment, it's like she's gone insane.' Without hesitation he ordered an urgent EEG. I couldn't thank him enough.

The results astounded and shocked the staff when they discovered she was suffering unusual brain activity that they told me had never been seen before. (I remembered hearing similar words when she was four years old when told about the brain debris). Chiara was now diagnosed as being in a constant state of seizure and rushed into High Dependency in a critical condition. It was midnight, approximately twenty-four hours after first calling the ambulance and all hell was breaking loose.

After two nights without sleep I was told Chiara may not survive, making me extremely angry at having been ignored for so long. With Dani at my side, the attentive and compassionate doctor suggested I call my husband and family for support. He explained a dangerous drug would need to be administered and her heart closely monitored if she were to be given any chance at all. There was no guarantee the treatment would be successful but there weren't any other options, giving me no choice but to agree.

With Chiara now an adult I was asked if I had Power of Attorney and Medical Guardianship over her. Thankfully I had been advised when she turned eighteen years of age to have it in place for her, as once a child reaches adulthood, a parent loses the right to make decisions on their child's behalf without that paperwork in place.

The doctor now in charge and the High Dependency staff were absolutely superb, a vast contrast to our experience with a few in the Emergency Department. A dutiful and very concerned nurse was constantly with us. Having to call Steve to tell him Chiara wasn't expected to survive was one of the toughest phone calls I've ever made. I was glad Dani was already there. If I had to ring her with the news it would have been even tougher. Steve arrived in the middle of the night after a three-hour drive from home.

A young female intern came in saying Chiara had a serious urine infection that had entered her bloodstream. It could threaten the shunts and she required immediate antibiotics. She went on to say, that as Chiara was running out of viable veins an intensive care doctor would be inserting a PICC line (Peripherally Inserted Central Catheter). A PICC line is a long thin tube inserted into a vein near the elbow and threaded into a large vein just above the heart.

The professor from neurology arrived with a team of interns and I queried the bloodstream infection. He looked at me puzzled then asked the female intern to 'read the numbers' to him. He then said, 'Those numbers don't tell me she has an infection. This could've simply come from another person handling Chiara at the time. Helen, she doesn't have an infection.' Had he not arrived when he did she would've had a PICC line inserted for no reason.

As the hours passed, Chiara slowly began to respond to the 'dangerous' drug, finally bringing the seizure activity under control. Immensely relieved, we left High Dependency and admitted to a ward where a bed was supplied for me as well. Chiara was ultimately diagnosed with Complex Epilepsy as there wasn't a name for the type of seizure she had experienced. It then took five hundred milligrams of Carbamazepine per day to successfully control it, and she would have to take it for the rest of her life.

A very tired Dani went home to her family returning to the hospital every day. Steve also left as he hadn't long started his new job at the local council and without holidays due, we couldn't afford for him to take time off. I remained at Chiara's bedside.

With the seizure activity controlled the focus turned to the baffling cause of the persistent abdominal pain. An X-ray revealed constipation and therefore deemed the cause of her pain. I kept maintaining it was something more sinister, as Chiara was often constipated but had never experienced such pain but I'm just a mother, what would I know?

I asked about appendicitis and ovarian cysts but I was instantly dismissed. The attending nurses said Chiara required a cruel G and O (Glycerine and Oil) enema at 2am to clear her constipation. I asked them to wait until a more reasonable hour as I wasn't convinced the pain was due to constipation. They didn't want to wait and tried to insert the enema but Chiara wouldn't co-operate. I again asserted they wait until later in the morning.

A neurologist was to be called to review Chiara but due to a nurse misreading the medical notes she requested an urologist instead.

When he arrived, he was confused as to why he'd been called and not a neurologist. As he was an urologist I thought he was the perfect specialist to discuss the abdominal pain with. He said that as he was there anyway he may as well try to help, and promptly ordered a CAT scan of her lower abdomen.

Once again everyone was left stunned. The scan revealed an 8mm kidney stone and I was relieved someone had finally shown enough interest to seek the cause of her excruciating pain. A stent was placed into her right kidney to temporarily relieve some of the agony, and an appointment made to return to hospital to have the stone blasted a couple of weeks later.

The incompetence continued from medications not being written up properly or not at all, to one nurse attempting to administer someone else's medication as she hadn't read the name properly on the label, and another arrived to give her a nebuliser because she had misread the medical notes that stated 'neuro obs' but she read it as 'nebuliser!'

It's the incompetence I have experienced from time to time across hospitals over many years, that renders me reluctant to leave Chiara's side. The problems we faced during some admissions was due to Chiara presenting with obscure indistinguishable symptoms but it doesn't excuse condescending attitudes or incompetent staff putting her life at risk.

Weary and energy depleted I have tried my absolute utmost on a day-to-day basis to ensure Chiara enjoys the best quality of life and the best possible medical care. The stress I suffer watching helplessly as she fights to survive never gets easier. The majority of staff we have encountered across numerous hospitals are superb, highly skilled, compassionate and caring professionals, while the ones who aren't make life difficult not only for the patient and their families but also for their colleagues.

Prior to Chiara's discharge I was strongly encouraged by staff to report to the Administration Department all incidences of incompetence we had been subjected to. Complaints lead to improvement and unless people speak up they cannot expect change.

# *Life goes on*

July 11 2008 marked yet another milestone as we celebrated Chiara's twenty-first birthday. After all she had been subjected to only a few months prior, it was all I could wish for to see her happy, healthy and enjoying her special day with her family.

I decided the perfect birthday celebration would be to return to Queensland to re-live the memories from her seventh birthday, many of which Chiara had not remembered. So with Dani and her partner Randal, along with Braeden, Tayah and Jai, we flew back to the Gold Coast of Queensland to celebrate Chiara's twenty-first birthday and gather more happy memories.

With my darling parents growing old and frail the decision was made to sell the family home and move them into a retirement village. My mother was happy to be moving into a brand new unit but it broke my father's heart. He always said he would only ever leave his home 'in a box' but unable to walk independently, constantly fracturing his spine due to osteoporosis, and both parents suffering interstitial lung disease, he finally accepted neither of them could manage the upkeep necessary to maintain their large home.

After all the times my parents had looked after my girls, especially the support they gave throughout my single parenthood and Chiara's

*Chiara age 21yrs*

ill health, it was time to start giving back. My parents were now the ones needing help so Chiara and I stayed with them whenever she was well enough, one or two nights most weeks, to do whatever we could for them. It was clear Chiara was wrestling with the reality of her adored grandparents' battle with old age, so I suggested she undertake voluntary work at the Women's and Children's Hospital once a week while I looked after them. She loved her volunteer work. At the same time she was studying some TAFE courses in the hope of gaining paid employment working with children.

Eighteen months later my mother, suffering depression, reached breaking point and could no longer care for my father alone, as he kept falling, fracturing his spine and a simple knock to any part of his body caused a massive bleed. Even though Steve and I insisted they move in with us, I couldn't convince them it was my turn to look after them. They didn't want to be a burden on any of their children and refused. I grudgingly drove my father to his new home in a nearby aged care facility. It was the most crushing thing I'd ever had to do for my parents.

After getting Dad settled, I didn't want to leave him. When he asked how long he had to stay there I told him he just had to get better before I could take him home. I left in tears and then visited on a weekly basis. I had removed his emergency alert button from around his neck and handed it to my mother insisting it was her turn to wear it or she would be coming home with me. It took a while but eventually she agreed.

June 16 2009 our family chain broke with the passing of my beloved father at the age of 90. While I was devastated but extremely grateful to have my dad for as long as I did, my two girls were absolutely shattered at losing their 'Bossy.' While trying to manage my own grief, Chiara required extra support to help deal with her deep sorrow. I wondered if she or Dani would ever recover from having to say goodbye to the most significant male in their lives who they loved dearly.

Chiara quickly spiralled into depression and it took a long time with extra love and care to help ease the overwhelming loss that affected her deeply. Chiara began having 'visions' again but now it was my father who appeared to her. At every family gathering since his passing, Chiara nudges me to say 'Mum Bossy's here' and he usually has a message for a particular family member depending on the occasion. Her visions and messages always bring us tremendous comfort.

There has been two other occasions in recent years, where Chiara has 'seen' a deceased person. One at a friend's birthday party where she recognised him as being her friend's father who had died a few years prior, and another at a family wedding, where she saw a gentleman she had never met but once again later recognised in a photo. On both occasions Chiara was given messages by the deceased to pass on to their loved ones.

# *Uncanny coincidences*

In December 2009, it was finally announced a second miracle had been accepted by the Pope. It was granted to a woman who had apparently been cured of cancer, leading to the canonisation of Mary MacKillop on Sunday 17 October 2010. Chiara and I travelled back to Penola to join the community in the celebrations. I can't explain it but we both feel at home in Penola.

During the canonisation celebrations in Penola, Chiara and I visited the Mary MacKillop Interpretive Centre located next to the little schoolhouse, that had opened since our last visit. While wandering through looking at everything, it was me this time who caught sight of a particular photo on the wall. The photo was apparently of a young Mary MacKillop. I was amazed at how much I thought the photo looked a little bit like a young Chiara.

Seeing the photo, spurred me on to do some research about Mary's life. So when we arrived home I bought the book that Father Paul Gardiner had written about Mary's life.

Based on what I have read in his book, the Sisters of Saint Joseph was co-founded by Mary MacKillop who set up orphanages and schools for the poor and underprivileged in South Australia, Victoria and Sydney. She also established convents, refuges and welfare institutions, opening her first school in a stable at Penola in 1866. Mary suffered a stroke and died in 1909 at the age of sixty-seven. Two miracles were eventually attributed to her and acknowledged and accepted by the Pope and Mary is now known as Saint Mary of the Cross MacKillop.

The more I read, the more I was surprised at some of the coincidences between her life and ours so I have included a few.

Joanna Barr Smith was Mary's close friend. My maiden name is Barr. Chiara's name is Chiara Jo Barr. When she was born I was very tempted to extend the Jo, to Joanna but concluded Chiara Joanna was too much. Had I done so, her name would have been Chiara Joanna Barr. Mary's remains are interred in a vault in her chapel in Mount Street, North Sydney where the tomb Chiara was drawn to and knelt transfixed is contained. The vault was a gift from Joanna Barr Smith.

Mary's father was Alexander MacKillop and his mother's name was Helen. Mary was named Mary Helen. My name is Helen Marie. I added the name Anne at my confirmation. Annie was also the name of Mary's sister and also my father's grandmother. Mary suffered ill-health most of her life, much of it gynaecological issues, just as Chiara too has suffered. Mary worked with children. All Chiara has ever wanted to do is work with children.

Mr Barr Smith gave Mary two thousand pounds to build the Convent at Kensington. Chiara's father gave me two thousand dollars that I used to take Chiara to the beatification. The convent Mary had built is located immediately across the road from where I attended school in Norwood, a suburb of Adelaide. There was something special about Mary's quaint chapel in the convent grounds but I never understood as a child why I sensed a connection and found so much peace within those walls.

Mary played piano and was a governess to the L'Estrange family. I learned piano at a private home in L'Estrange Street. It would be even stranger if that street was named after the same L'Estrange family.

Mary was employed for a time by stationers Sands and Kenny. My parents owned businesses and next door was a stationery shop owned by a Mrs Sands.

My father and his siblings were taught by the Josephite nuns, so too myself, three siblings and in turn my two daughters.

My parents thought it strange when they were given a large photo of Father Julian Tennyson Woods back in the 1970s. Many years later they donated the picture to the Sisters of Saint Joseph at Kensington. I recognised a photo in the gallery in Penola that looked identical to the one they gave.

Pregnant with Chiara I had initially settled on the name Cameron if she were a boy. For approximately two years Mary lived with a family in Penola bearing the surname Cameron. Dani and I lived with a lady named Heather Cameron for approximately two years in Norwood.

Cardinal Patrick Moran thought Mary was worthy of a sainthood. A Patrick Moran lived next door to my Grandparents. The investigation into Mary's life with a view to canonisation was initiated in 1926. My mother was born in 1926.

In 1860 Mary came to live in South Australia. One hundred years later in 1960 I began schooling at Saint Joseph's Memorial School, Norwood (a school also related to Mary MacKillop's journey) and later attended secondary school at Mary MacKillop College, Kensington, South Australia.

In 1863 Mary lived in a rented property named Bay View House. In 2001 my husband and I had our dream home built on Bellevue Circuit which could only be accessed via Bay View Parade.

When Mary made her first religious vows, a woman named Clare Wright also received her 'habit.' I worked with a Clare Wright at Shergis Hairdressers.

A good friend of Mary's was named Father Hughes. One of Chiara's specialists was Dr Hughes. Another friend of Mary's was Teresa, and another Annette. My sister's name is Teresa Annette. A Margaret Mary Sexton was with Mary on board the 'Wakatipu.' One of my father's cousins was named Marie Sexton.

There is mention of a Dr Campbell and a Dr Higgins. Our family doctor when we first moved to Yorke Peninsula, was Dr Campbell and

Dr Higgins was one of Chiara's doctors at the Women's and Children's Hospital.

When I finished my draft manuscript I knew I would need permission to use photos of Mary MacKillop, so I searched the internet for the appropriate contact details. Yet another uncanny coincidence lies in the surprise I received discovering the Chairman of the Board of Mary McKillop Care South Australia was none other than Mr Jim Birch who had been the Chief Executive Officer at the Women's and Children's Hospital. He was the one who listened and acted upon my grievances during his reign all those years ago.

I found it somewhat eerie to read what I consider to be uncanny coincidences, and there may be more if I ever get the time to sit and read Fr Paul's book of Mary MacKillop in full.

# Sudden accidents change lives

August 2012 our already financially demoralised lives suddenly changed direction when Steve suffered a serious and permanent back injury at work that rendered him unable to return to his job. An appointment with a neurosurgeon resulted in him being told there wasn't anything that could be done for him. Although in excruciating pain, on a multitude of medication, unable to sit, drive or stand for long, as well as being informed he would probably never work again, changes to the welfare system meant Steve didn't qualify for a Disability Pension at that time even though I was considered his Carer.

Instead, he was placed on the unemployment benefit – Jobsearch – otherwise known as 'the Dole' and expected to look for work. Now *his* life had become one step forward, two steps back, interwoven with WorkCover, Centrelink, TAFE and Personnel Placement Disability Services while trying to survive financially. We were both psychologically at breaking point despairing over how much more we could endure.

September 2012, in the early hours of the morning my mother fell in her bedroom breaking her hip and leg. With a simple press of that annoying little button she was able to automatically notify my brother Greg who in turn phoned me. An ambulance crew quickly arrived having been alerted via the button and after administering pain relief, whisked her off to hospital for surgery.

A week later the doctor delivered the news she required permanent High Care and couldn't return home. Keeping my siblings informed I set about finding the best facility. As happy as we were with the wonderful care my father received at the aged care facility he stayed at until his death, I didn't want Mum to go there. I thought it would be detrimental to her psychological health.

Looking for a facility for Mum was made easier with all the research I had done in the two years leading up to my father requiring care. I asked her doctor if she could be transferred by ambulance explaining I had taken my father to his Nursing Home and couldn't go through it again. He agreed to make the arrangements and I met Mum at the facility. Relieved I wouldn't have to worry about her living on her own anymore brought with it the realisation of losing our free accommodation, and the use of her car whenever we had to fly Chiara to Adelaide. Life wasn't getting any easier but at least Mum was well cared for.

# *Intuition ignored*

November 2014 at the age of twenty seven, Chiara was suffering severe pelvic pain. I was suspicious it was the endometriosis reappearing so I took her to her gynaecologist and asked him to book her into hospital to perform a laparoscopy. Although unconvinced with my diagnosis, he agreed to my request. The hours passed and it was clear she was in trouble as I waited, pacing the hospital room.

Chiara was full of endometriosis and a nodule had attached to her bowel. In the process of trying to remove it, the gynaecologist perforated her bowel. He immediately ceased the surgery and called for a bowel surgeon to urgently repair the damage. Antibiotics were administered to protect Chiara's shunts from infection. I was left completely shocked as I was only expecting the results of the laparoscopy and to take her home the same day, not to hear she was in intensive care after undergoing major bowel surgery.

Five days later she was discharged but instead of improving, deteriorated. A five-hour round trip to revisit the gynaecologist a few days later resulted in more antibiotic medication and him declaring she was fine. We returned home but my intuition was screaming shunt and I was worried. Within days I called an ambulance and we were taken to the local hospital where the Royal Flying Doctor was called to fly her back to Adelaide. Re-admitted into hospital, the intensive care team and gynaecologist were recalled to review her. Everyone was baffled as to what was wrong. The bowel surgeon was also summoned. His visit was brief and he too declared she was 'fine.'

Thankfully the intensive care team were unconvinced and discussed Chiara's medical history with me. The gynaecologist claimed it was common for women to suffer like Chiara after endometriosis surgery. Having been a sufferer myself until cured with the hysterectomy, his statement was unacceptable to me. Chiara was noticeably very ill and exhibiting intensifying shunt symptoms. At my request the intensive care team agreed to commence neurological observations.

The gynaecologist had the weekend off and in his place Dr Ian Jones was looking after Chiara. I was surprised to see him. He was Mr Hanieh's neurosurgical registrar twenty years prior and was familiar with Chiara's childhood history and how quickly she can deteriorate. He said he had learned to listen to me years ago. He had also helped Dani at a Medical Centre when she had a severe reaction to Maxalon, and had since changed his profession to become a gynaecologist.

I became increasingly distressed as the days passed, knowing without doubt we were facing a shunt issue. On his return from a weekend break her gynaecologist continued to insist she was 'fine' ignoring my concerns. I didn't appreciate his flippant attitude. When Chiara cried and said 'Mum he thinks I'm putting it on,' I immediately took control and had her discharged from the private hospital. I wanted her to see Dr Vrodos at the Flinders Medical Centre. A decision that possibly saved her life.

Whilst I had total confidence in the staff at the private hospital, and especially the intensive care team, Chiara and I had lost all confidence and respect for her gynaecologist. Arriving home with a very sick daughter I immediately rang Dr Vrodos who booked an MRI scan which took place in Adelaide two days later. The results didn't reveal a shunt malfunction. We travelled back home with me still convinced there was something wrong with the shunt.

By 10.30pm that night Chiara wasn't able to move and was in agony. I called an ambulance. It took until 2am for the officers to stabilise her for the twenty kilometre trek back to the local hospital. Once there the doctor on duty recalled the Royal Flying Doctor to take her back to Adelaide, where an ambulance transported her from the airport to Flinders Medical Centre.

I left Chiara in the care of the local hospital and at 6am without sleep, I began the three hour drive to Flinders Medical Centre while Steve waited by the phone at home. Living approximately two hundred kilometres from the Adelaide hospitals, I prefer him to stay home to care for Chiara's little dog so she knows Coco is well looked after in her absence.

With my mother in the nursing home I would be without a car unless I drove my own down. Chiara had to travel in the plane for the first time without me, then transferred to an ambulance in Adelaide and she was frightened. The ambulance arrived with her on board as expected at 9am and together we were whisked into a private room in the Emergency Department at Flinders Medical Centre.

It was an unexpected and much appreciated relief to experience the high level of care and personal attention Chiara received while in the Emergency Department. It had improved substantially since our last visit. I pondered whether the complaint I had lodged had been acted upon. We were still in the Emergency Department at 10pm waiting for Dr Vrodos who was still in the operating theatre.

With Chiara getting worse by the minute and spiking a temperature, I was convinced she was battling a shunt infection as a direct result of the perforated bowel. I asked her nurse to contact Dr Vrodos. Unable to leave his patient on the operating table he sent his assistant who immediately ordered blood tests.

A shunt infection confirmed Dr Vrodos booked her in for surgery to take place at midnight. Seriously ill and very weak, grasping my hand tightly, it broke my heart when Chiara whispered, 'Mum I'm really scared. Dr Vrodos hasn't operated on me before. I know I'm dying and if he doesn't help me soon it will be too late.' I held her tight for a moment and then briefly left the room so she wouldn't see me sobbing.

After regaining my composure I returned a few minutes later to reassure her. I had enough confidence in Dr Vrodos to know he would save her life and she would soon be well again. Without sleep for two consecutive nights I was fast slipping into my zombie mode battling to function when Dr Vrodos appeared at Chiara's bedside. He came to discuss the surgery and consequent necessity for an external shunt while treating the infection. He reassured us he would take good care of her and have her feeling better. He left to prepare for the operation.

Frightened and unable to relax it was the first time Chiara was administered a sedative to help her settle before surgery. Five hours later I received a phone call from Dr Vrodos saying the operation was a success. It was evident to me that the infection diagnosed as E-Coli, had without doubt come from the bowel perforation.

Steve had booked a cabin for me in a nearby caravan park. In tears of relief I left to finally get some sleep. It was the first time I couldn't stay by Chiara's side as being in the adult world there wasn't always a bed for me. I just had to trust she would be well looked after.

The next day when Dr Vrodos came to visit, Chiara put her arms out to hug him while she was lying on her bed and whispered, 'Thank you for saving my life.' Dr Vrodos reassured her he was there to help any time she needed him and explained that as she no longer needed the shunt in her brain stem where the cysts are, he was able to remove it for her. It meant one less shunt to malfunction leaving her with just the one in her fourth ventricle. It was the second time the shunt in the cysts had been removed. We hope this time it will be permanent.

A week later with the E-coli under control Chiara returned to theatre to have the remaining shunt re-inserted. It was placed into her chest instead of the peritoneal cavity in order to protect it in case she should require future pelvic surgery. With her history of endometriosis, further surgery was inevitable.

Well enough to return home bearing fresh scars to heal, Chiara was discharged on Christmas Eve much to everyone's relief but our ordeal was far from over. Six weeks after the initial endometriosis\ bowel surgery, we returned to the gynaecologist for her post-operative check-up. Chiara entered his office with multiple scars clearly visible on her partly shaved head. She was very weak having lost approximately fourteen kilograms since we last saw him. He didn't appear concerned, other than to apologise for perforating her bowel, to which I responded that I am well aware there are risks in any surgery, and Chiara told him it was okay.

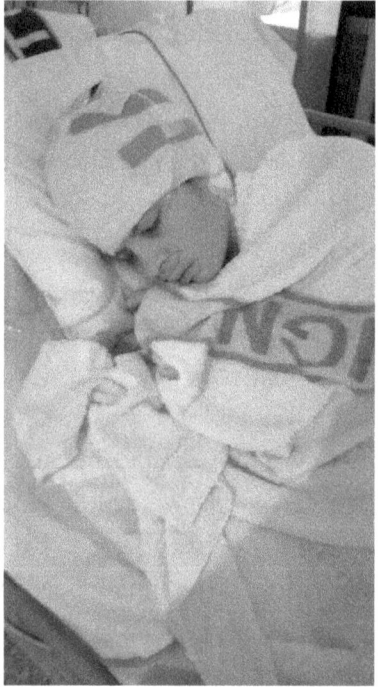

*Chiara after Surgery*  *Chiara with an external shunt*

We had forgiven the perforation as being one of the risks but not his attitude of fobbing us off when we were trying to convince him she was very ill. He had made Chiara feel that he believed she was 'putting it on.' When we left his rooms Chiara said she didn't want to go back to him anymore because of his attitude, and I was pleased to oblige but it meant seeking out another gynaecologist and I didn't have Dr O'Loughlin to advise me.

Many years prior, when Dr O'Loughlin informed me that he was retiring, I had asked him to recommend a gynaecologist for Chiara in case she ever needed one. The person he recommended never seemed to be available, and was often interstate, so I had to seek out another gynaecologist for her. She was very happy with my choice at that time and for approximately ten years under his care so his attitude surprised us both, especially when he insinuated she was 'putting it on.'

As a result of the E-coli and potent antibiotics to kill the infection, Chiara has been left with multiple food intolerances. Able to eat and enjoy any foods she desired prior to the bowel perforation and E-Coli, now she can't tolerate gluten, dairy, soy, fructose or lactose without experiencing pain and nausea, and she has also developed an allergy to nuts.

Chiara enjoys cooking when she's well enough and with the aid of a few new appliances, she is able to create meals as well as ice-creams, spreads, breads and desserts using only the ingredients she can tolerate; many we had never previously used or heard of. It was pitiful seeing her so painfully thin but unable to tolerate all the fatty foods I used in my wiz bang milkshakes I made for her in the past - to help her gain weight - there was nothing I could do. We've been to doctors, specialists, dieticians, nutritionists and a naturopath and all have said it will take a long time to recover, if at all.

# *Planning a future*

On 5 October 2010 Dani and Randal presented us with their own little miracle, Ashton Samuel. A fourth grandchild for me to cherish, and another nephew for Chiara to spoil. Dani married Randal on 24 January 2015, which gave Chiara only a few weeks to convalesce. She was excited to have a happy occasion to look forward to, knowing she would be spending the day with those she loved, especially her sister and much adored niece and nephews.

The tenderness and compassion her niece and nephews show their Aunty Chiara is heartening and commendable but not surprising from such sensitive and very protective children. They share a bond that sees them devastated whenever Chiara is hospitalised.

Knowing she had an important responsibility to take care of gave Chiara the incentive she needed to get well. Although frail and unsteady, with eternal thanks to Dr Vrodos, she was able to sign her sister's marriage certificate and enjoy the wedding celebrations.

\*\*\*

With my mother settled in her nursing home, she directed the proceeds of her home be equally divided between her four children. It was

*Chiara signs Dani's Wedding Certificate
and is excited to see Braeden, Tayah, Jai and Ashton*

enough for me to purchase a beautiful caravan and vehicle to tow it, so thanks to my beautiful mum, I now have affordable accommodation anytime Chiara is hospitalised. It has made a massive difference only paying for a caravan site, and not motel or cabin fees, sometimes for weeks at a time. It has also enabled us to take Chiara on short holidays in between hospital trips.

By 2018 with no hope of ever working again, Steve finally qualified for the Disability Pension and with the benefit of my having taken out Total and Permanent Disability Insurance on him when he first started working for the Council, our financial situation finally improved.

We are now selling our beach house in order to buy what Chiara calls her dream home, complete with a magnificent river view.

With her now at the age of thirty-one, she had considered moving out of home, so we looked into and considered supported accommodation but it proved to be an extremely difficult and daunting task. Chiara soon realised it meant she would have to live with a number of people and wouldn't be able to tolerate the noise level and so decided she would be much happier staying with Steve and I. When the time comes that I am no longer able to care for Chiara, Dani will step into my role as her guardian and advocate, and together will decide the best on-going living arrangements.

Meanwhile to give her a little independence and me some peace of mind to go for a walk or visit a friend, Chiara reluctantly agreed to wear one of those annoying little alert buttons to enable her to stay home on her own for short periods. Technology has helped my sanity in many different ways over the years, from the pager to mobile phone then the loan of the laptop to get this book started and document her life, and now that little button.

# *Fighting for improvements*

I haven't lived the South Australian public hospital system as a long term consumer for the past three decades without witnessing and learning a thing or two along the way.

When Chiara was born in 1987 and spent her first one hundred and one days in the Queen Victoria Hospital, she was under the principal care of Dr Vigneswaran. All doctors working within the paediatric nurseries communicated for the best possible outcome for Chiara and her tiny room-mates. They worked as a team and always endeavoured to keep families fully informed. At no time was I ever concerned about a lack of communication or the quality of her treatment.

It came as a shock therefore to discover a dire lack of communication in other hospitals. I found myself co-ordinating Chiara's care and passing on vital information between specialists, registrars and therapists; not an easy task. The greatest frustration was when doctors wanted to change or add to her treatment without consulting each other.

One particular issue was when a doctor who wasn't in the neurosurgical field, was about to prescribe and administer medication he believed would control the hydrocephalus but hadn't discussed it with

Mr Hanieh. When I asked Mr Hanieh about it he told me it doesn't work. I returned to the doctor to tell him he was not to give it to her.

Having often observed an obvious lack in communication, I pondered whether a program could be implemented whereby patient information could be accessed via a small computer at each bedside enabling easy communication between doctors.

When Chiara was admitted to a ward at Flinders Medical Centre in 2008, I was amazed to see each bed had been equipped with an overhead computer. I was informed the computers were to enhance communication while doubling as a television and personal computer for patients. Disappointed to see doctors weren't using them I asked one of the nurses why, only to be told the system was fraught with problems.

In conversations with other parents over the years, it became evident many found the lack of communication frustrating, leaving them irritated and confused. There was also a significant issue with 'red tape,' where too often there was an excessive amount to cut through, yet in other areas, not enough.

I couldn't believe the amount of ridiculous red tape and the number of staff the request had to pass through, when a mother simply asked for a larger size nappy for her child in the children's hospital. I went and found some for the child myself, in another ward, after seeking permission from the deputy director of nursing to do so, who agreed the process needed simplifying, and thanked me.

Visiting hours and patient privacy at the children's hospital was a simple example of insufficient red tape. It irked me that a large board bearing all the patients names was in full public view. A person decides who walks through their door at home but in hospital it was open slather.

I mentioned to Administration about the lack of privacy and how it could possibly put a child's safety at risk, and was very pleased when the board was moved into the side office, out of public view. Someone must have agreed with me.

For some patients and their families, visitors with noisy and unruly off-spring can be nerve-wracking. Parents and immediate family must have open access but in my opinion, and experience, young children should have set visiting hours, at least in the Neurosurgical ward.

\*\*\*

'Re-engineering' is a productivity and service improvement concept recognising the need for returning to basics and restructuring corporations. I firmly believe it is the direction in which our hospitals should all be headed in order to rectify, and in turn, improve the quality of communication and services. If ever there was a case for it, I believe it is within our deficient and very sick health system.

A multi-million dollar building with a fancy façade does not save lives or allow the delivery of services that are expected of a world class hospital. It takes technology, equipment, manpower and enough beds necessary to operate at their full potential in order to save lives. Australia often leads the world in research and technology yet funding is continuously cut.

While Governments perpetually slash funding, our hospitals continue to degenerate and patients suffer needlessly. I have seen nurses frustrated at the lack of basic essentials, such as thermometers, vomit bowls, etc., wasting valuable time searching for items in other wards. I have witnessed babies forced to share necessary equipment such as heart monitors.

As I continued to present the management of the Women's and Children's Hospital with grievances relating to the basic requirements of sick children and their parents, some management staff and committee members admitted they were oblivious to a number of inadequacies and safety issues affecting ward staff, patients and parents\care-givers. They sat and listened but most of all treated me with respect and appeared to appreciate my input, and have acted upon numerous suggestions over the years.

I had explained my situation, and included the fact I was a single parent without a partner to help with such things as finding carparks near the hospital. Most times Chiara took ill during the night which involved presenting to the Emergency Department then having to ask someone to look after her while I left to move my car, as the parking area only permits 'drop offs.' Parking anywhere near the hospital was limited to two hours. Without a visitor's carpark on site, I was forever touring the streets of North Adelaide looking for long term carparks.

Once the car was parked I then had to walk alone and frightened through dark streets back to the hospital often in the middle of the night. I begged many times over the years for a carpark to be built, and for permits to be issued at a much reduced rate for parents requiring long term parking. I kept telling anyone who would listen, that it would pay for itself in time, by creating an on-going extra income stream for the hospital.

It took a few years but not only did we parents get a carpark we managed to get two, with the added bonus of discounted parking permits. The old underground one was upgraded and opened to the public, requiring only a few gold coins on entry, and a multi-storey car park was built directly across the road from the main hospital entrance.

Today those carparks would be taken for granted. It was a massive effort over many frustrating years to get them built and I sincerely thank hospital management for listening to all my whinges and trying to improve facilities for parents, in order to help them cope with all the unnecessary stresses.

It took until the year 2003 to finally have an Magnetic Resonance Imager (MRI), the ultimate in scanning technology, funded and installed at the Women's and Children's Hospital. It is with grateful thanks to the generous and untiring hospital supporters, and the then McGuiness McDermott Foundation, who raised one million dollars, which was matched by the South Australian Government. In September 2018, the new Prime Minister of the Liberal Government casually announced thirty new MRI Scanners would be purchased to boost the number of bulk-billed machines in public hospitals, at a cost of $175 million. Apparently, they will be delivered to areas deemed to have the greatest need across Australia. Finally, and thankfully, a politician 'gets it' and to think I fought so hard all those years ago, just to get one for the children!

Improvements continue to evolve and when parents' retreats on wards were promised, I smiled to myself. The hospital had come a long way since the day a cleaner abused Dani for making Chiara a piece of toast for breakfast in the staff kitchen. However, any consideration given to a long-term patient, and parent's psychological state in any hospital, while dealing with the trauma unfolding within hospital walls, remains questionable. We have lived the health system for more than three decades, yet neither Chiara nor I have ever been offered any counselling to help us cope in a world of pain and suffering we don't recognise as normal.

Numerous times I heard, 'only a miracle' could save my baby, yet I was left abandoned to deal with pulverising emotional stress with nothing more than the offer of a box of tissues, a pat on the back and sometimes but rarely, a cup of coffee. The vast majority of medical and nursing staff across all hospitals we have attended were, and are, superior but they are there to save lives and deal with the needs of their young patients. They cannot be expected to have the time or skills to help parents deal with unmitigated, soul destroying grief.

Many years ago during a Consumer Consultant meeting, the Head of the Social Work Department became aware of our plight. She invited me to talk to Adelaide university students to help them gain an insight into the reality of life with a very sick child. I was given the title Senior Lecturer in Professional Competence. I hope our story has helped.

# *Euthanasia*

While I fear the realisation of legalisation allowing voluntary euthanasia, it is more about how and when it is administered and who decides, rather than the act itself that disturbs me. I don't believe in prolonging life using drugs and force-feeding patients when a person is in a vegetative state beyond hope of a quality recovery.

In my opinion, even though euthanasia would be deemed voluntary under the law, with the continuous decline of our health system it is worth considering the possibility our dedicated doctors may, in time, be dictated to by Government. They may lose the right to heal their patients if those patients are deemed a drain on the country's finances.

There is potential for the floodgates to open and we may then have to justify our right, or our loved one's right to live. It will take a person's fight for life to a whole new level. How will premature babies and those born critically ill or challenged at birth, the physically and intellectually disabled, the aged and the frail all fare under a cost-driven government or greedy family members?

What if it had already been legalised the day a doctor came to me when Chiara was four, to say that 'doctors' who were unknown to us and outside of the Women's and Children's Hospital wanted to pump Chiara full of pain-killers and let her die? She wouldn't have stood a chance and I would not have had a say. Chiara is alive after having fought hard and stands testament to the excellent care and attention she received from doctors dedicated to saving lives.

As I see it 'voluntary' euthanasia is a decision to commit suicide assisted by a doctor who would in my opinion, be expected to perpetrate murder. If euthanasia follows, how will any of us be safe? Palliative Care is already in place to relieve the suffering of the terminally ill. With a health system continuously in decline what a great way for Government to save millions of dollars by bumping off the sick. Why willingly give them that right?

Many declare euthanasia is dying with dignity but what dignity is there in being put down like an animal? It apparently can take fifteen minutes to die when euthanized as the body slowly shuts down. Evidently the person is first paralysed and then injected with a special cocktail of lethal drugs. How is that a dignified way to die? Who has ever been able to tell us what it's really like so others could be warned what to expect. It could be a very long and excruciatingly painful and terrifying fifteen minutes. It's enough to scare a person to death!

I would prefer a vegetative patient be administered increasing doses of drugs such as Morphine until they pass away naturally, instead of force fed foods that keep them alive. Some would argue that is no different to euthanasia but I prefer to think of it as being kept comfortable and letting nature take its course.

While on my soapbox I believe people in the final stages of terminal illness should not be resuscitated. I can understand if an otherwise healthy person has suffered a heart attack or asthma attack for example, being resuscitated but why compel a person without a glimmer of hope to return to continue suffering more pain and perhaps be in an even worse state than before.

Why would anyone want to be resuscitated to suffer more of the same and the promise of worse to come? Why resuscitate only to then tell an already deeply distressed family their loved one doesn't have long to live or that they'll need to decide when to pull the plug? Allow the person to die once, naturally and with dignity.

EPILOGUE

# *An extraordinary journey*

As of 2018 Chiara has undergone fifty-two rounds of neurosurgery as part of her life but the one operation that she has battled to come to terms with, is the hysterectomy. After suffering horrendous pelvic pain over many months, Dr Jones agreed to investigate and was shocked in 2017 to discover the mangled mess she was in. There was no alternative but to do a complete hysterectomy, leaving Chiara devastated at the prospect of never being able to bare children, something she is still struggling to come to terms with.

MRI's probably number in excess of thirty. More than one hundred CAT scans, along with numerous shunt function studies and X-rays. Anaesthetics would exceed sixty. After tolerating so many intravenous drips, blood tests and needles she barely has a viable vein left. Thank God for Medicare, Private Health Funds and Ambulance cover as I would never be able to afford Chiara's care without it.

Giving birth twelve weeks too soon to a grievously ill baby, then watching her fight through unbearable suffering to live a life most take for granted, has been more horrendous than words on paper can describe. I don't know how she continues to smile through insidious pain or how she takes it all in her stride without complaint, accepting life as perilous as it is.

The Endocrine Clinic became involved after concerns were raised about Chiara's growth. A therapy involving hormone injections six days a week for the rest of her life was suggested. I resolved not to go ahead with that therapy. I didn't trust the long-term effects and Chiara had more than enough to contend with without subjecting her to daily injections. Thankfully, the decision proved to be the right one as she grew steadily, and although short, has reached a reasonable height.

Looking at her today and how well she looks, makes it difficult to believe all that she has endured but her battle-scarred body is a daily reminder of her gruelling journey. Her scars make it difficult to forget all she has survived, all the twists and turns, trials and tribulations endured along the way, interwoven with fun and laughter, miracles and apparitions. Chiara doesn't remember most of her early years, the good or the bad while I will never forget. I long for a normal existence for her, free from surgery, blood tests, drips, drains, MRIs, CAT scans, EEGs, shunt function studies, anaesthetics, sutures, seizures, emergency trips to hospital and the occasional, frustrating encounter with egotistical staff.

Living on the edge from the day I was admitted into the High Dependency Unit at the Queen Victoria Hospital in 1987, to Chiara's first few seconds of life and every moment of every day since, has been exhausting and stressful but we have been extremely fortunate. One thing that has never changed is the fact Chiara continues to need a set of eyes on her, as her health can quickly deteriorate without warning.

I'm grateful to have both my exceptional, beautiful darling daughters, precious, healthy grandchildren, a supportive husband, step children and a close knit family, so I cannot ask for more. I don't take any day for granted; conscious of the fact life can change in an instant, and be taken without warning.

Our time-bomb existence continues with Chiara and I both worrying about the fact I'm not getting any younger. The older and more tired I get, the more we worry for her future without me as advocate, co-ordinating her everyday care at home and during hospital admissions. To wallow in her debilitating, painful condition however, is energy wasted.

Although Chiara will never be able to gain a licence to drive a motor vehicle, she is making the most of what life has to offer. With me as her taxi driver, she has worked voluntarily at the Women's and Children's Hospital, local schools and cafe and takes part in Leisure Options and Living Skills programs when she is well enough.

Enjoying a thirst for knowledge it's not surprising watching her devour books and study TAFE courses. She has proficient computer skills, often doing her own research. Chiara's ultimate dream is to acquire a position working with children, while neurosurgery and hospital visits are interruptions accepted as part of life.

Over the years, many different government departments specialising in the disability field, have wasted many hours interviewing us, only to have Chiara written off as an 'un-met need' on every occasion. As a result, to date we have not received any physical assistance from any department. Recently the Australian government introduced the National Disability Insurance Scheme and Chiara has had her 'plan' approved. We live in hope.

A gentle, compassionate and articulate soul she enjoys cooking so I created a social media site for her, specialising in multiple food intolerance recipes. Chiara creates the recipes, trials them for taste, photographs the successful ones and posts them to her page knowing she is helping others. The following is a link to Chiara's facebook page. https://www.facebook.com/Easy-Recipes-for-Multi-Food-Intolerances-1719700574977069/

***

Many people won't, don't, and will never believe Chiara has visions and I don't expect them to. I am however grateful some have been privileged to witness mysterious events with us along the way. It leaves me feeling comforted even though I can't comprehend any of it.

Through rare and random conversations over the years, I'm surprised how many people have admitted to me they too have seen deceased souls yet remained silent through fear of derision, and being labelled as schizophrenic, as some including Chiara, have. Apparitions more commonly referred to as visions, are a gift I wish everyone had. A gift to be respected not mocked or labelled as a mental illness.

On the day Chiara was born I turned to my grief-stricken mother and promised her someday it would all make sense but born gravely ill and enduring a life-time of pain and suffering will never make sense.

With all the heartache, physical and psychological exhaustion, I am privileged and honoured to play such a major role in Chiara's life. Hydrocephalus at its debilitating extreme I can only hope is now behind us. All we can do is pray it will never again cause the relentless tribulations of the past. Chiara has beaten it at its worst thanks to Mr Hanieh, Dr Vrodos and no doubt Divine Intervention. As her mother I live in hope someone somewhere will find the ammunition crucial to annihilate the hideous hydrocephalus monster, forever rendering it incapable of destroying lives.

As I finally recognise the need to offer Chiara's inspirational story, I reflect back to Dr O'Loughlin's initial request made in 1991. He wanted to know how I was still sane. My answer would be much the same today. If indeed I am still sane, it is due to the incredible support I have received over the years, from medical and nursing staff, family and very special friends, along with the fact that I still have my two beautiful daughters and of course, modern technology.

When I began writing, I initially titled my manuscript One Step Forward Two Steps Back; words I have often used throughout Chiara's life struggles so it seemed appropriate. Our paranormal and inexplicable journey relating to visions, apparitions, and Mary MacKillop, was never going to be included through fear of ignorant mockery and ridicule until I realised Chiara's story had become as much about Mary MacKillop and her miracles, as it did about her.

While Chiara's story continues - with some days more difficult than others especially when she collapses without warning - I realised if I don't stop writing now, I may soon be too old to remember I ever started, and her story thus far would never be told.

Through the intercession of Mary MacKillop, Chiara has by her mere existence, inspired the doubtful and encouraged many, while restoring faith in some, and given absolute confirmation to myself and others that miracles really *do* happen.

I stand beholden to Saint Mary of the Cross MacKillop, indebted to many, and regardless of what is in store I know without reservation…*it could be worse.*

*Saint Mary of the Cross MacKillop*
*Trust in God*

# *Thank you*

Chiara's journey, although challenging, would have been exceptionally more confronting without the dedication and support of an extraordinary group of committed and devoted medical and nursing staff across a number of South Australian hospitals.

Heartfelt and sincere thanks go first and foremost to Mr Hanieh. Words cannot express the impact such a beautiful, brilliant man had on our lives. What you did for us went far beyond the call of duty. Chiara meant as much to you as she does to me and I shall be eternally grateful to you and your family who accepted the continuous disruptions to their lives as you fought to save others. Life has not been the same for us without you in it. We never had the chance to say goodbye but you will live forever in our hearts, our souls and our minds. Until we meet again, goodbye for now our treasured friend.

Dr Vigneswaran, without you Chiara wouldn't have survived that first hour and the following one hundred days. Our support from you didn't end the day we left the Queen Victoria Hospital. You too bore the devastation as Chiara's battle to survive continued. Our last conversation only days before your passing, was about the need for this book, and that you would help me to find a publisher. To your family, I say thank you for your support of a truly wonderful man in his endeavour to save the lives of our special delicate tiny babies. Dr Viggy helped me keep my sanity and hope during the days spent at the Queen Victoria Hospital. His sudden passing devastated us and his spirit remains forever in our hearts.

Dr John O'Loughlin, the best gynaecologist obstetrician and friend I could have wished for. A massive thank you goes to you. Without your ongoing care and continued support I would never have been able to conceive Chiara. You were always there for me over many years and surgeries and I treasure the special bond we shared. Thank you for encouraging me to write Chiara's story, even though it has taken more than thirty years to write to the final chapter.

Dr Nik Vrodos, how do I thank you for welcoming us into your life, for saving Chiara's and my sanity and for the respect you showed to us both since the day we met. Your patience and constant reassurance kept me going through some of Chiara's darkest days as an adult, and helped her & I both cope. Thank you.

Dr McCusker thank you for saving both our lives on that desperate day and for your patience and understanding I so desperately needed throughout those horrific moments. Thank you for giving me my little daughter, and congratulations on a job well done. Drs Sweet and Mollison thank you for your kindness and understanding through such a traumatic time.

Drs Ross Haslam and Andy McPhee, sincerest thanks for all you did for us and for your ongoing support. Drs Lamb, Rajadurai, Henschke, Metz, DeMarie, Tapp and Barlow heartfelt thanks to each and every one of you.

To the Neo-Natal Intensive Care Unit, Special Care and Premature Unit staff at the Queen Victoria Hospital particularly July - October 1987. Your devotion and dedication had to be seen to be believed. It was a world where angels existed. Deepest thanks go to each and every one of you.

To Mr Hanieh's registrars based at the Women's and Children's Hospital 1987 - 2005 especially Drs Chris Barnett, Paul Hammond, Ravi, Elizabeth King and Ian Jones a massive thank you.

Sr Jan Ramsay, Ros Schwarz, Dr Judith McMichael and the Long Term Follow Up Team. Anne Leahy thanks and appreciation for all you did for us and the support you gave along with the High Dependency Unit and nursing staff on the 5th and 6th Floors of the Queen Victoria Hospital in 1987. You gave much appreciated exceptional care and attention.

Professor Simpson, along with Intensive Care staff Women's and Children's Hospital, especially Drs Neil Matthews, Gavin Wheaton, Greg Delbridge and Carol Khaw, a special thank you and to all the staff based in Fielders, Duncan and Rose Wards thank you for caring not only for Chiara but for me as well.

Drs Des Dineen, Narang, Dave Sainsbury, Tomkin, VanderWalt and a special team of anaesthetists, thanks and gratitude for your continuing tolerance, patience and respect shown to Chiara and me. Theatre and recovery staff, especially Helen, Michelle and Mandy for your kindness, unwavering support, understanding, and all the tissues. The orderlies for their gentleness, respect and patience during numerous trips to Theatre.

Further thanks and gratitude are extended to:

Dr Morony and his team in Nuclear Medicine and radiologists especially Graham Truman.

Dr's Richard Couper; paediatrician, Dr Penfold; Endocrine Clinic, Dr Lane and Dr Pater; Eye Clinic. Drs Manson and Abbott; paediatric neurologists, and Dr Goldwater and his awesome team of microbiologists and Dr Weekes; hypnotherapist.

The physiotherapists, especially Peng Ha and Fiona, speech pathologists, dieticians and occupational therapists.

Jan Volkmer, secretary to Mr Hanieh and caring friend to Chiara, Dani and myself. Thank you for all you did for us and for understanding every time Chiara took over your desk and computer.

Women's and Children's Administration staff, especially Jim Birch, Jan Macklin and Halina Laver for putting up with grievances and acting upon them. Marjorie Santich in Child Psychiatry you were an amazing help to both Chiara and me.

Fathers Farmer, Zerafa, Boylan and Vin Reagan (Society of Jesus) all sadly deceased and Fr Kevin O'Loughlin thank you for all your support through the toughest days at the Women's and Children's Hospital.

Thank you to the patient staff of the Royal Adelaide Hospital MRI unit.

Drs Gil Blicavs, Becky Jeanes, John Leaney, (deceased) and Maitland Medical Centre General Practioners and hospital and office staff, past and present, especially Drs John Campbell, Georgina Moore, Kwabena Duah, a massive thank you all for your care and attention.

St John and Ambulance SA officers and the Royal Flying Doctor Service thank you for your extraordinary care.

Neurologist Dr Tom Kimber and physician Dr Maria Della Malva, heartfelt appreciation and thanks for taking over Chiara's adult care. Dr Siddons, medical and nursing staff at the Flinders Medical Centre and Flinders Private Hospital, Memorial Hospital and Calvary Hospital a massive thank you.

Ms Rae Craddock, public relations/fundraising officer supreme, a sincere thank you for your extraordinary support and friendship.

Humphrey B. Bear try as I may I cannot find the words to express that which is in my heart. You achieved what medicine, equipment and technology failed to do and for that I shall be eternally grateful.

My deepest gratitude is extended to everyone connected with the 'Make a Wish' Foundation especially Elizabeth, Nicola, Charmaine and Robyn. Thank you all for the special memories you have given us. Thank you for making a child's dream come true and for caring enough to give freely of your time to change the lives of others. It was the most exhilarating holiday we have ever had.

Di, at the then Bavarian Steak House on the Gold Coast, a thank you seems so little for so much. We will never forget that fantastic highly emotional evening. Thank you for all you did for us.

Guest Relations at Seaworld, Dreamworld and Movieworld and to each and every person who went out of their way to see to it, that not only Chiara had a memorable time but Dani and I also. Richard and the Con-X-ion bus service a special thank you and Shangri-La boat cruises, the Currumbin Bird Sanctuary and all on the Gold Coast, thank you for making our week so perfect and your incredible much appreciated support of the Make a Wish Foundation.

To all the dedicated people working quietly without recognition behind the scenes in all the hospitals, medical centres, ambulance and Flying Doctor services to ensure my daughter, and the sons and daughters of Australian parents and visitors to our country make the fastest and best possible recovery.

To the Reporters of Channel 10, Channel 9, Channel 7, The Sunday Mail, The Advertiser, Messenger Press and the now defunct The News for continuing to show interest in Chiara's progress over the years, which in turn, helped me raise awareness and much needed funds.

Liz (deceased) and Ros, Wynn Vale Kindergarten 1991 thank you both for your patience understanding and help in making Chiara's Kindy days so memorable indeed.

The children, parents and teachers of St Francis School Wynn Vale 1992–99 especially Mark Shadiac, Dawn Parkinson, Julie Sypek, Belinda Bennett, Julie O'Nions, Deb Madgen, Kris Maka and Marilyn Maloney for accepting Chiara into your school and into your hearts. Thank you for allowing her to grow in mind and spirit and be educated within your close knit community.

Pat Terminello, Sister Margaret, students and staff Mary MacKillop College Kensington, sincere thanks. Thank you to Sheena and the Catholic Education Department and Fiona and the devoted team at Townsend School, for all your support.

George Holt, Chiropractor, our sincerest thanks to you for what you have done for Chiara and me over the years.

To all the 'hospital mums' especially Deb MacQuillan, Louise Neaylon and Helen Tremayne. We all shared a bond that can never be broken regardless of where we are in the world at any given time. If anyone understands the pain and suffering it's you, my special friends.

I apologise for any names spelled incorrectly.

*A thank you is not enough but it is all I have to give*

# *Glossary*

| | |
|---|---|
| Beatification | The Pope's recognition of a deceased person having performed a miracle |
| Bradycardias (Braddys) | Dangerously low heart rate |
| Brain haemorrhage | Bleed on the Brain |
| Canonisation | The Pope's recognition of a deceased person having performed two miracles that may proceed to Sainthood |
| Carbamazepine | Seizure control medication |
| Electroencephalogram (EEG) | A test to detect abnormalities of the brain |
| Hydrocephalus | Water on the brain |
| Meningitis | Infection in the brain |

# Glossary

| | |
|---|---|
| Nebuliser | A machine commonly used to treat asthma which administers a mist of medication into the lungs. |
| Novena | The reciting of powerful prayers for a special request\miracle over nine consecutive days often performed by groups of people at the same time. |
| Peripherally Inserted Central Catheter | A PICC line is inserted into one a vein near the elbow and threaded into a large vein just above the heart. |
| Phenobarbitone | Seizure control medication |
| Pneumonia | Lung infection |
| Pseudomonas | A Blue\Green pus like infection |
| Septicaemia | Blood poisoning |
| Sixth Nerve Palsy | Nerve weakness resulting in pulling the eye towards the nose |
| Tegretol | Seizure control medication |
| Ventricular Peritoneal (VP) Shunt | Fine tubing resembling cooked tubular spaghetti used to drain fluid from the brain to the stomach cavity |
| Ventricular Atrium (VA) Shunt | As for ventricular shunt except draining into chest cavity |

*I have never asked*
*'Why us'*
*for I know*
*for this to happen*
*to us*
*it can happen*
*to anyone*

*Chiara October 2018*

www.ingramcontent.com/pod-product-compliance
Lightning Source LLC
Chambersburg PA
CBHW062242300426
44110CB00034B/1238